All Kinds of Papercrafts

ALL KINDS OF PAPERCRAFTS

John Portchmouth

with illustrations by the author

Studio Vista London

To my family

With my thanks and appreciation to Michael Glass for photographing
the work, and to Sue for typing and checking the script and for
her support throughout the preparation of the book

Text and illustrations copyright © 1972 by John Portchmouth
All rights reserved.
Photoset and printed in Great Britain by
BAS Printers Limited, Wallop, Hampshire
First published in Great Britain by
Studio Vista Publishers
Blue Star House, Highgate Hill, London N19

ISBN 0 289 70300 X

Contents

1 Where to begin

Once upon a time (as historians would probably forget to mention) a certain wizard was walking under a tree when a leaf fluttered down past him and fell to the ground. He stopped to pick it up and held it in the palm of his hand, considering it for a while. He turned the leaf this way and that, and rolled it slowly round each of his fingers in turn; then, closing his hand on it and whispering an unpronounceable word, he tossed it up into the air. At once the leaf changed into a small green bird that rose on its wings and flew off to the sun.

A few people will say that such days are over now, and that this sort of thing could not happen any more. But could it? At this moment probably there is a boy somewhere who is folding a sheet of notepaper into a dart: in a second he will send it shooting across the room. Tomorrow he may make a boat from the cover of a magazine and launch it down a flooding gutter, or set it rocking on mountainous bath water; or he will blow up a bag to make the flat paper round and tight and ready to burst. Somewhere else a wedding guest is throwing a handful of confetti and watching it fall into a many-coloured pattern on the church path.

Like the leaf that the wizard found, paper may seem at first sight just flat and still. But as the leaf came alive in his hands, so can paper. With a few movements and a little uncomplicated magic, it can be changed into something completely new.

Everyone has seen paper behave in strange ways: a newspaper billowing and spinning across a park; a crumpled potato crisp packet unfolding itself when it is released; pages of a book curling in the sun; or an edge of blotting paper drawing water upwards from a bowl. Paper responds to wind and heat and water and to everything done to it. When it is pulled it tears in ragged lines or, if it is crêpe, stretches unbelievably. It stands on end when it is rolled into a tube; it tightens to a drum if it is damped and secured by its edges. There is almost no end to the things it can be made to do, and what it does by itself. It is both the simplest and most co-operative material to work with.

Almost anywhere one happens to be, at home or outside, there it is! Though it may be lightly disguised as magazines, comics, writing pads, food and parcel wrappings, circulars pushed through the door, tissues, carrier bags, typewriter carbons, exercise books, timetables or paper towels—still, underneath the disguise, it is only paper. It is handled and used more than almost any other material, yet it is probably thought of mainly as reading matter, as something to write or draw on, or for putting to an everyday practical purpose. One may see a lump of clay or plasticine and think, 'Ah, I can make something out of that'; or come across pieces of fabric, old cartons and boxes, bits of wood, and other found objects and say, 'That would be just right for a model or picture.' Yet these are rarer than paper. Does paper offer the same chances for invention? There is much more of it—some new, some used or thrown away—and there is an incredible variety of colours, textures, patterns and shapes waiting to be discovered. Perhaps it is worth investigating.

It might understandably be thought that only good quality paper such as drawing or craft paper is suitable for making things. For certain work, they are: but any sort of paper can be used as well. Each has something about it that can give a start. It does not matter that there are pictures or print on it, that it is creased or torn, or that it seems too large or too small. These may be the very features that can start a thought moving.

This book examines ways to express imaginative ideas through all kinds and conditions of paper, using it alone or as the principal material. There are notes on beginning and carrying out a work, and supporting illustrations; but rather than giving step-by-step instructions, which could only end up in one way, the author has chosen to indicate where searches lie and to leave the reader to his own adventures—with a little help where it might be welcomed.

2   The paper

The best way to start looking at papercraft is to look at some of the types of paper we come across almost every day, and at some that are not so common. There will be many alternative colours and textures for several of them and a variety of shapes and sizes from confetti to long, continuous rolls. The examples of the different types of paper that follow are only a few of those that the reader is likely to discover for himself.

Thin, lightweight papers

Tissues; airmail letter paper; rice paper; Bible paper; filter paper; crêpe paper; typewriter carbons and thin copy paper; paper towels; confectionery wrappers; imitation Japanese printing paper.

   These papers are flimsy: any small breeze disturbs them and sets them in motion, lifting, floating, fluttering, whirling. They are so responsive that they seem to have a life of their own. They crumple easily and tear at a touch: cutting seems almost unnatural to them. The moment they are damped or pasted they go limp and can be modelled softly over other forms or moved about flat under the hands into swirls and ridges. Any paste sticks them. Many of them are transparent against the light or when they are wet: tissues, for example, become very transparent when they are pasted to a surface, but lose this effect again when they dry. (They remain transparent if they are stuck down with a polyurethane varnish instead of paste.) In some of the papers, like tissue and type-writer carbon, the colour is not always fast: pasting them makes it run into surrounding areas. This can produce some lovely results, flooding colours softly into each other; and, although it is not always certain what will happen, the effect can be partly anticipated. Tissues may also fade in the light. Any of these papers can be made up into soft, light forms of their own, though generally needing the support of a stronger material.

Slightly heavier papers

Newsprint; kitchen, shelf or lining paper; blotting paper; writing and thick typing paper; office duplicating paper; detail paper; sugar, pastel and construction paper; wallpaper; frieze paper; paper bags; magazines; book paper; gummed labels; light wrapping paper; tracing paper; printing paper; corrugated confectionery wrappers; cellulose cleaning paper.

   These are a little thicker and not so immediately affected by move-ments around them. They still crumple easily, though with harder creasing than the flimsy papers. Tearing can leave them with either straight or ragged edges, and they lend themselves to cutting. They can be rolled and folded more firmly, and keep their shape better when they are damped or pasted. Most of them can be modelled wet over other forms, and worked into different effects on a flat surface. Any paste sticks them. Some, like tracing paper, are more or less transparent;

others, like pastel paper, are not, and would cover up any surface underneath. The colour in some of the papers fades after a while in the light, and it is worth testing a few samples by leaving them in the window for a week or so before using the paper for anything you want to last. All the papers can be made up into fairly firm shapes on their own, sometimes without support.

Papers with greater strength

Cartridge and heavy drawing paper; poster paper; prepared water and oil painting paper; stout wrapping paper; photographic paper; chart and map paper; manilla paper; carrier bags.

On the whole, these are tougher and heavier papers. Greater pressure is needed to crumple them. They are harder to tear, but cut cleanly. They can be rolled, folded and creased sharply to keep their shape, and can be made up into all kinds of forms with no further support. Damping only affects them slowly, and then with little distortion. Because of their thickness, they often need a heavy duty paste or a stronger adhesive to stick them, though ordinary paste may still do it satisfactorily. For the most part, they are quite opaque, and any colour is reasonably fast.

Marked, patterned or textured papers

Ruled and graph paper; fancy wrapping paper; wallpaper; leatherette and wood veneer paper; book end-paper.

These papers could be light-weight or strong, depending on the purpose for which they were made. Their characteristics will correspond to those listed above. Their markings or pattern may be faint or bold, and can often be incorporated effectively into a design in contrast with plain papers.

Papers that have a resistance to damping

Waxed paper; vinyl wallpaper; bitumen impregnated paper; metal foil paper; greaseproof paper; machine glazed wrapping paper.

All these papers are damp-proof to some extent, some more so than others. Some are fairly light-weight, others heavier and stronger. They are useful where the work is likely to be affected by outside moisture, as in wind-vanes, or when it is used with a wet medium, as in stencilling. Any colour is usually fast.

Papers that are more or less transparent

Some of the light-weight papers; tracing paper; greaseproof paper; cellophane.

In some of these transparency varies between the wet and dry states and according to the source of light. Cellophane and some of the thin plastic papers, both clear and coloured, are very transparent under most conditions, and enrich with their own colour any surface they are laid or pasted over. Sheet gelatines can also be freely used in papercraft. The colour is fast.

Paper that has been made up into special shapes

Doilies; paper table-ware; confetti; streamers; food and other packaging.

There is an ever-increasing variety of manufactured paper products for practical or decorative use in the home, for display in stores and public places, and for festive occasions. They come in all kinds of weight, thickness and transparency. Some, like doilies, are figured with pierced designs that can create interesting surface effects either by themselves or cut up and reassembled in some way with other papers. Some, like hanging decorations, are quite ornate and intricate in construction. Others, like confetti, are simple, but can be very useful for certain effects.

Matt papers and shiny papers

Matt papers such as blotting and pastel papers have a dull, often rough surface, and do not reflect the light. Shiny papers, such as glossy magazines and metal foil paper, are smooth and reflect more light. Some papers have just a dull sheen. Contrast between the different kinds can contribute to the effect of a work.

Paper can be obtained from any number of sources, including offices, printing works, paper mills, packing and despatch firms, newspaper offices, home decorators' stores, stationers, confectioners, photographers, art and craft shops. It can take the form of used packaging, newspapers and other household waste, party decorations, old exercise books and other unwanted books and magazines.

Each paper has its own character and way of behaving. You will discover, in handling it, what it suggests and what you can make with it: the effects you achieve will be different for each paper you use. Each kind of paper is both the starting point and the means of carrying out a work. The imagination guides and the hands control what happens.

3 Main processes and tools

Much paper work can be done with the hands alone, and it is mainly through turning and shaping paper in this way that a feeling for it begins to grow. The use of tools, however, can take experiment further and give a fresh stimulus to invention. Ideas can often develop from noticing the effect a certain tool has on the paper. Processes that recur in various parts of the book are explained in this section and a selection of tools is given for carrying them out. You should refer back to this for information as necessary.

Tearing

If a piece of paper is too large, or you want to remove a part from it, the first thought probably is to tear it: paper itself suggests this. What happens can always be something of a surprise. The tear never goes quite as planned, and leaves unexpected edges. In a creative context this can contribute as much to the work as the quality of the paper itself.

Different kinds and thicknesses of paper tear in different ways—some cleanly, others with a ragged or furry edge. This characteristic can be used to varying effect and bring a touch of adventure to designing with paper shapes. If you hold the paper at one point and tear it across without moving your hold, one kind of paper may tear in random directions, another in a straight line; and variations may be noticed by tearing from different sides of a sheet. A thicker paper could separate in layers along part of the tear, leaving unevenly thick edges. If you follow a tear along with your hands, you can control its direction. Even finer control is possible by tearing between the finger or thumb nails. Tearing shapes from a variety of thin and thick papers will give you an idea of what to expect.

Cutting

Scissors: long- and short-bladed scissors; pointed surgical or nail
    scissors; pinking shears
Craft knife: there are different shaped handles and blades designed
    for various purposes. Use the ones you can manage and which
    do the job best. Some tools have interchangeable blades. Useful
    knives include (fig. 1a) Leipzig, (b) Swann-Morton, (c) X-acto,
    (d) Stanley, and (e) a linoleum cutter.
Cutting board: a renewable sheet of cardboard pinned to a drawing
    board is useful—also pinboard, linoleum or hardboard (masonite)
Metal straight-edge; ruler
Scissor sharpener; carborundum stone
Guillotine (paper cutter) with guard

The cut edge is more precise than the torn edge, and the cut-out shape has a different character from the torn one. Cutting may feel more natural with some papers than others, but there are bound to be times when a process or a design calls for sharp-edged shapes. The kind of work you are doing will suggest whether you should use scissors or a craft knife for this.

using scissors
Use long- or short-bladed scissors depending on the length or intricacy of the cut. If you are cutting with long-bladed scissors, take advantage of the whole length of the cutting edge, and re-enter each new cut along the direction of the line or it will be jagged. Pointed scissors are essential for details, for starting a cut from a point within the paper area or for ending it accurately at a line or point. There are certain scissors, such as pinking shears, designed for special cut effects: ordinary scissors can produce irregular effects by varying direction during cutting.

using a craft knife
A good craft knife is really vital. It is useful for making continuous straight or curved cuts, for removing shapes from inside an area, for precision work, and for cutting through several layers of paper held firmly together. Always have a board of some kind under the paper. Make sure you are using the cutting edge of the knife: it is not always clear at first glance with some kinds. Draw the knife towards you in a continuous movement. If you can practise doing this freehand you will find you soon develop quite an accurate control. For greater accuracy with straight cuts, use a metal-edged ruler; in cutting returning curved

Fig. 1

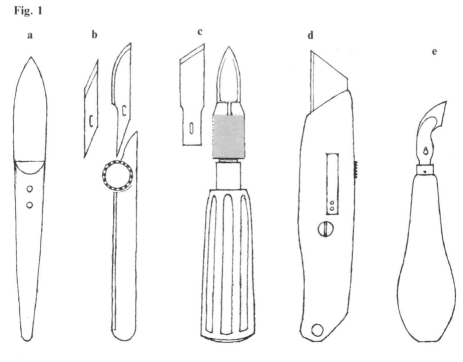

a b   c   d   e

lines, turn the paper rather than twist the blade or change position.

Keep both scissors and craft knife sharp. You can get a small sharpener for scissors at most hardware stores, though the blades will need re-grinding occasionally. To sharpen a craft knife, work both sides of the blade backwards and forwards on a carborundum stone at the angle of the bevel. Moisten the stone with a little machine oil. Be careful to preserve the tip of the blade as this is important in detail work and a burred tip would cause the paper to tear.

using a guillotine

If you have to cut or trim large quantities of paper, it is best to have a guillotine with a guard for the blade. To cut at right-angles to the edge, line the paper up with the top edge of the guillotine platform and bring the blade down in an easy, continuous movement, not in jerks. To cut at any other angle, mark the paper at the two ends of the cut, and line these up with the blade edge of the platform. A good guillotine will have a spring-loaded batten parallel to the blade by which you can hold down the paper: this is really essential if you are cutting several sheets together. It should also have an adjustable batten which you can set for regulating the width of paper you cut off.

a toothed cut (fig. 2)

You can give paper a toothed edge with just a single cut. Roll the paper and cut it across at a low angle: it opens out with a wide toothed edge. By rolling the paper tighter or cutting at a steeper angle, you get a sharper toothed effect. If, instead of making a single cut across, you make a V-shaped cut, the teeth are closer together. The effect can be

Fig. 2

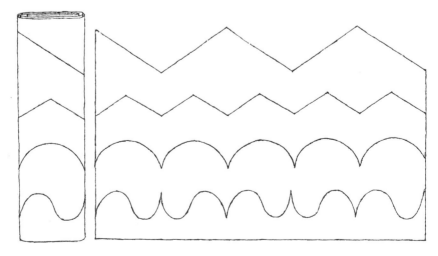

varied in countless ways by making different kinds of cut, e.g. by cutting in a curve across the roll. Try cutting a simple arc, a full half-circle, and an S-shaped cut, and see what has happened to the edge when you unroll it. Then try other cuts of your own.

Measuring

Sharp pencil
Eraser
Ruler
Compasses
Divider
Set square
Protractor
T-square

Much creative work with paper can be done without a measuring tool of any kind: your own judgment may be quite enough. Use such tools only when you have to: they can hinder your inventive handling of the materials if you come to rely on them.

You will, however, probably need them for processes involving accurate cutting and assembly.

Folding, creasing and shaping

Bone folder
Ruler or straight edge
Table knife—blade or handle
Handle of a fork or spoon
Lollipop stick
Any similar smooth-ended tool

The success of papercraft often depends on sharp folding and creasing, especially if you are making up shapes from the paper. Firm papers fold and crease better than flimsy ones. Turn the paper over along the line where you want the fold, and press along this line from the most convenient point, sharpening the crease with the finger tips, the back of the nail or with a tool. Press the crease over a piece of clean scrap paper if there is any risk of your craft paper marking. Lightweight papers crease quite easily. Heavier ones can be lightly scored first. Do this with the tip of a knife or a similar tool. Press gently to avoid cutting into the paper. Very thick papers will only crease sharply by scoring first.

To put a curved crease in paper, score along the line of the curve and work carefully round it, bending the paper up or down to get the effect you want. You can raise paper into all sorts of interesting formations by scored creasing and develop your discoveries with more effect as you see what happens.

Here are some useful folds and curves that may be combined in different ways:

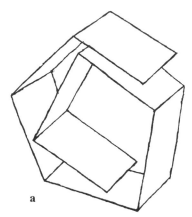

a

Fig. 3

roll-over fold (fig. 3a)
Lay a sheet or length of paper flat. Starting at the edge nearest to you, fold a strip upwards at right angles to the sides and press out to a sharp crease. Fold the strip again up the same side of the sheet and continue doing so until you reach the top. It unfolds rather like a scroll. The distance between folds increases slightly as you continue to roll, especially with thicker paper. You should allow for this.

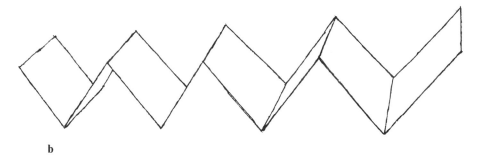

b

zig-zag fold (fig. 3b)
This is like the roll-over fold, except that you reverse the paper for alternate folds. Lay a sheet or length of paper flat. Fold a strip upwards from the near edge at right angles to the sides and press out to a sharp crease. Turn the sheet over and fold the strip again up the new side. Continue in this way, turning the sheet before making each new fold until you reach the top. It opens out into a regular zig-zag or screen fold. You can make the strips different widths or fold them at various angles to the sides. Judge visually as you go along, or, if you need to be more accurate, measure and mark the edges of the paper, and fold across from the marks.

battlement fold (fig. 3c)

This is a further development of the last two folds. Lay a sheet or length of paper flat. Fold a strip upwards from the near edge at right angles to the sides and press out to a sharp crease. Fold the strip again up the same side of the sheet. Turn the sheet over and fold twice up the new side. Continue in this way, turning the sheet after every two folds until you reach the top. It opens out with a regular battlement fold. You can vary the width and angle of the strips as in zig-zag folding.

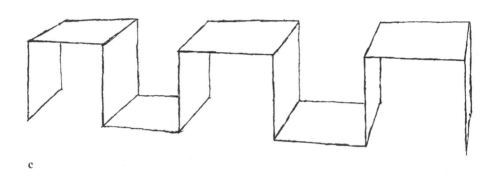

c

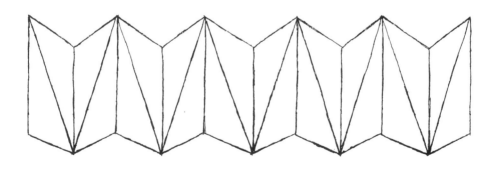

d

arrowhead fold (fig. 3d)

Lay a sheet or length of paper flat. Make a zig-zag fold and press out the resulting shape. Fold the shape diagonally across from two of the corners, and press out to a sharp crease. Open the sheet. Accentuate the creases so that they face alternate ways. The paper will now stand or lie in arrowhead folds.

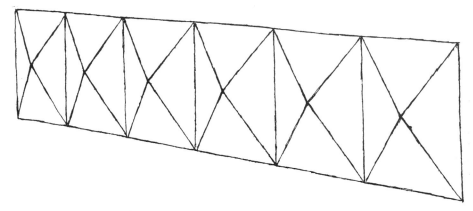

diamond fold (fig. 3e)

Lay a sheet of paper flat. Make a zig-zag fold and press the resulting shape out flat. Fold the shape diagonally across from two of the corners, and press out to a sharp crease. Do the same from the opposite two corners. Open the sheet. Accentuate the crossing diagonal creases so that they all face in one direction—either up or down from the dividing vertical creases. Care is needed to bring the diamond shapes out clearly.

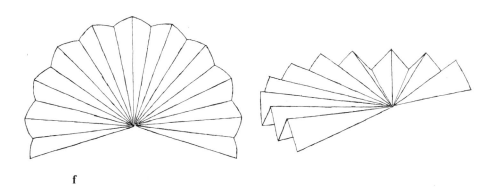

f

fan fold (fig. 3f)

Cut out a circle of paper and mark the centre. Depending on how shallow or deep you want the folds, estimate and mark lightly at intervals round the circumference the width you can allow for each full fold. Cut straight from one of these marks to the centre. With the paper flat, turn up the cut edge to meet the next mark along, and press out sharply from the centre, making half the fold. Turn the circle over and complete the fold by lining up the first half exactly with the edge underneath. Press out sharply again. You now have a full fold. Turn the circle over and turn up the fold to meet the next mark. Press out sharply from the centre, making half of the second fold. Turn the circle over and complete the fold as above. Continue in this way making the rest of the folds until you get back to the cut. Open out the fan. The depth of the folds will vary according to how far you open it.

You can also produce a fan by making regular zig-zag folds in a strip of paper. With the folded shape flat on a table, bring the two sides round towards each other, fanning out the folds from the centre. Glue between folds where they meet at the centre.

four-pointed star (fig. 3g)

Cut out a square of paper. Lay it flat. Fold it in half lengthwise and crease sharply. Open it out. Fold and crease it in half the other way and open it out. Turn the square over. Fold it in half corner to corner, crease it sharply and open it out. Fold and crease it corner to corner the other way and open it out. Press the paper in gently from the sides to form a four-pointed star.

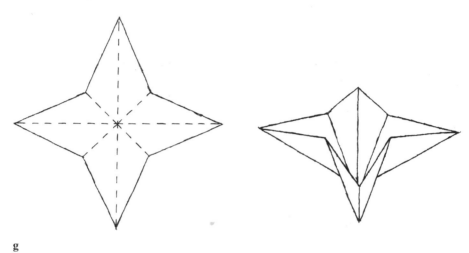

g

six-pointed star (fig. 3h)

Describe a circle with compasses. Keeping the compasses set to the same radius, use them to make six equidistant marks on the circumference of the circle. Join the marks with straight lines to form a hexagon. Cut out the hexagon and lay it flat. Fold a pair of opposite edges together and crease sharply. Open out. Fold and crease the other two pairs similarly. Open out. Turn the hexagon over. Fold two of the opposite corners together and crease sharply. Open out. Fold and crease the other two. Open out. Press in gently from the sides to form a six-pointed star. Stars with eight or more points can be made in the same way.

h

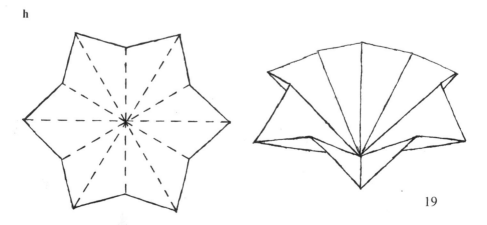

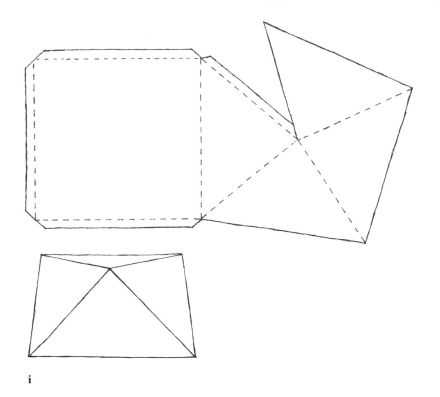

i

pyramid (fig. 3i)

Draw a square for the base. On one side of the square, draw an isosceles triangle. This will be one side of the pyramid. Its height when erected will be rather less than the drawing suggests. Draw a circle using the apex of the triangle as its centre and one of the sides as its radius. From where the base line cuts the circle, mark off the length of the base a further three times round the circle. Join from mark to mark with straight lines, and from each mark to the centre. There are now four joined triangles with a common apex. Draw flaps as shown and cut out the shape. Score along the dotted lines and fold the pyramid to shape. Glue the base flaps in turn to the inside bottom edges of the pyramid, and glue the side flap inside finally to close the form. If no base is needed, omit this from the plan.

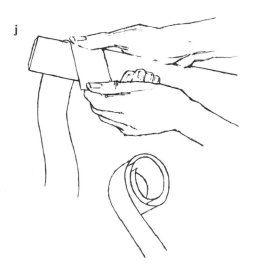

j

curl (fig. 3j)

Firm paper like cartridge or drawing paper develops a remarkable springiness when it is stretched and released. Cut a strip. With one hand, hold the end of it between the thumb and a ruler or straight edge. With the other hand, draw the strip down smoothly and quickly: the paper will curl inwards. Repeating the process tightens the curl. By this means, the curl may be made relaxed or tense. The paper will keep this shape, or return to it when it is opened out and released again.

wave

If, instead of pulling it straight through, you pull the paper through in short bursts and turn the strip over after each pull, the paper will take on a continuous wave form. It will retain or return to this form in the same way as a simple curl.

cylinder

You can often roll paper quite simply by hand to the shape you want or you can wind it round a cylindrical object such as a rolling-pin or a container instead. If the paper is dampened, it will hold its shape after drying: keep it in place round the object temporarily with an elastic band or by other suitable means. Secure the roll firmly with a thin line of adhesive down the meeting edges.

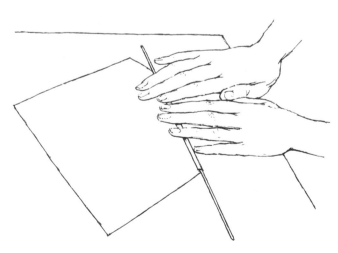

k

paper rod or stem (fig. 3k)

Lay a sheet of thin paper flat on the table. Lay a straight-ended knitting-needle diagonally across the near corner. Tucking the first roll round the needle, continue to roll the paper and needle together across the table until the roll reaches the thickness you want. Keep the paper tight round the needle all the time. Trim off any excess paper, withdraw the needle and secure the edge of the paper with a touch of adhesive. The shape will now remain rigid.

l

cone (fig. 31)
Draw and cut out a circle of paper. Make a straight cut from the circumference to the centre. Pass one straight edge over the other until the cone is the required depth (a small overlap produces a shallow cone; a greater overlap a deeper one). Allowing for just a narrow overlap of the two thicknesses, mark the sliding layer at the bottom edge of the cone. Cut from the mark to the centre, trimming off the surplus. (This shape can be a guide in cutting any further cones. Cut more paper away for a deeper cone and less for a shallower one.) Run a little glue down the overlap and hold the edges together until it has set.

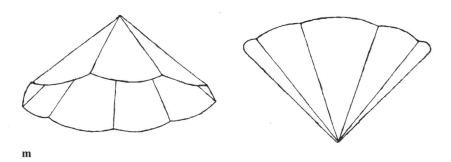

m

flat-sided cone (fig. 3m)
Draw and cut out a circle of paper. Cut the circle to make a cone as described above, but do not glue it yet. Allowing for a flap $\frac{1}{8}$ in. wide along one cut edge, divide the circumference equally into the number of sides the cone is to have. Draw straight lines from these points to the centre and score along the lines. Press out the creases sharply, bend the cone round to shape, and glue the flap.

Pasting and gluing

paste
Cellulose or cold water paste; a prepared paste
Mixing bowl
Paste brush or spreader

You will use paste quite a lot if you are doing a variety of paper work, especially for sticking large pieces flat.

Cellulose paste dries out without leaving any marks and stays fresh for several days. A little of the powder goes a long way: read carefully the amounts recommended on the package. Pour water into the mixing bowl and sprinkle the powder slowly on the surface, stirring from time to time until all the specks have gone. The paste will thicken considerably and be ready to use.

Ordinary cold water paste tends to mark slightly the surface on which it dries, and does not keep fresh for as long as cellulose paste. Add the powder to the water slowly, stirring all the time, until the correct consistency is achieved—not too thick, not too thin. It is ready for immediate use.

It is important to have the correct size of brush for pasting: if it is too large for the job, paste may be deposited on the wrong parts of the paper; if it is too small, it will be difficult to cover the whole paper before the paste begins to dry off, and some areas of paper may be missed altogether. An ordinary bristle paint brush is suitable for most work with cellulose and cold water paste. There are many sizes and shapes from which to choose and the more expensive ones should be avoided. Brushes made of hair are also useful for pasting along lines and covering small areas. In addition, there are special flat paste brushes (fig. 4a),

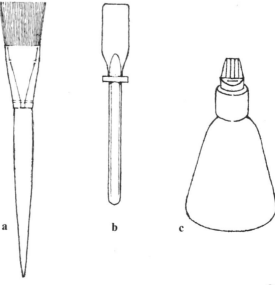

a   b   c

Fig. 4

often made of nylon. It should be stressed that the larger the area, the larger the brush needed to paste it. The best for big jobs is a decorator's brush—either soft or coarse and available in widths of up to about 6 in. Useful widths are 2 in. and 4 in. Take care not to leave the brush standing too long in the paste while not in use, and wash and dry it thoroughly afterwards.

Some of the prepared pastes that are sold in containers are better applied with the brush or plastic spreader provided (fig. 4b–c).

Clean scrap paper should be kept handy for putting the work down on. With small pasting jobs, be careful to paste only the meeting parts, or surrounding areas will be stuck too. If a large sheet is to be pasted, lay it flat on clean scrap paper and paste broadly and evenly in all directions. Work outwards across the edges so as to avoid dragging paste underneath them and getting it on the wrong side of the paper. Be sure to work over all the paper thoroughly, especially edges which can be missed in places. Paper invariably stretches when it is pasted, so wait a few moments before turning it over and laying it in place. Lift it carefully by the edges, supporting it underneath if necessary: it could tear if it is rather large or soft. Lay it in place and press it out gently from the centre under a sheet of clean scrap, working any air bubbles or paste lumps smoothly to the edge where they can escape. Keep the paper as flat as possible while it is drying.

Some papers, such as tissue paper, are too soft to take paste. It is better in these cases to paste the supporting surface and lay the paper onto it, working it down smoothly with the hands or a brush.

other adhesives

Gum, in bottles or jars, sometimes fitted with their own spreader caps (fig. 5a)

Liquid glue, in tubes with a nozzle, or in other containers for use with a plastic spreader or brush (fig. 5b)

Impact and flexible adhesives, in tubes or containers as above. These are mostly quick action adhesives that are effective both with papers and with heavier materials. Read the instructions on the container

Dot glue pen for applying spots of glue (fig. 5c)

Powdered, crystal or cake glue

Polyurethane varnish (clean the brush with a turpentine substitute)

Self-adhesive tape

Gum strip

These will all give a stronger or faster bond than paste, especially with thicker papers and other supporting materials.

To prepare powdered, crystal or cake glue, soak it for a while in cold water before adding it to hot water in a glue pot (fig. 5d) or similar container (a tin can in a pan of water will do). Keep the glue hot. Use an ordinary bristle brush or a special one reinforced with wire (fig. 5e). Clean the brush in warm water after use.

If you are using self-adhesive tape and need a great many small lengths for one job, cut them all beforehand, fixing them by their ends along a convenient table or shelf edge.

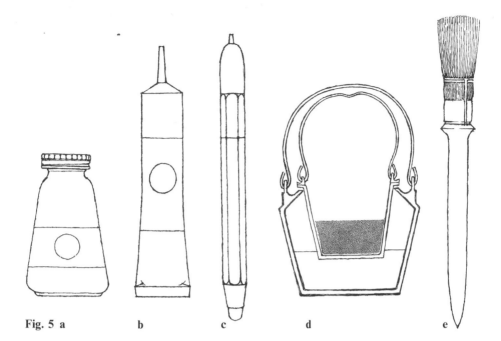

Fig. 5 a   b   c   d   e

Piercing

Awl (for card, pinboard, insulation board and similar materials)
   (fig. 6a)
Bodkin
Darning-needle held in a cork (fig. 6b)
Hand drill (for hardboard, Masonite, wood and similar materials)
   (fig. 6c)
   Papers or supporting materials may have to be pierced for fixing or
hanging purposes. Avoid enlarging the hole more than absolutely
necessary.

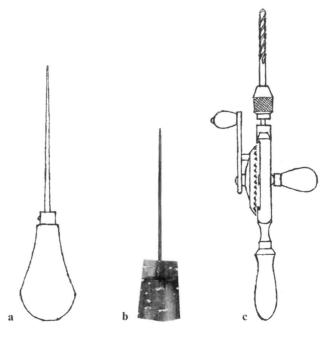

Fig. 6   a   b   c

Fastening

Dressmakers' pins
Thumb tacks
Paper clips and fasteners
Bulldog and foldback clips
Staple gun
You will sometimes want to hold work in place temporarily or fix it in position without gluing. It may also need to be attached to a support, e.g. as a hanging form.

Drawing and marking

Chalk, white and coloured
Charcoal in thin and thick sticks, soft or hard
Crayons: Conté and Terrachrome crayon; pencil crayon; wax crayon
Waterproof inks in black, white and a range of brilliant colours
Pastels, soft or hard; oil pastels
Pencils, soft or hard
Pens: felt tip pens that make dense bold lines and fibre tip pens
    that make dense fine lines, both in several colours, waterproof or
    water-based; ball point pens; steel nib pens; mapping pens
    All of these may be used for preparatory drawings or marking out the paper for work. They can also be used for drawing onto the completed shapes, giving them definition or detail.

Painting

Water colour
Powder colour
Poster colour
Acrylic or polymer colour
Decorators' emulsion paint
Coloured inks
Dye
Oil colour and thinners
Polyurethane varnish, matt or gloss
Size
Brushes and other means of applying paint (see below)
    Most colour in papercraft comes from the colours of the papers themselves. The wide range available should provide any effect you want, and this way you are more likely to retain the feeling of the paper. There may be times, however, when the paper or the support needs to be painted.
    Water colour, coloured inks and dye are clear and transparent and have most effect on white or light tinted paper. Waterproof coloured inks are particularly useful for rich detail painting. Powder and poster

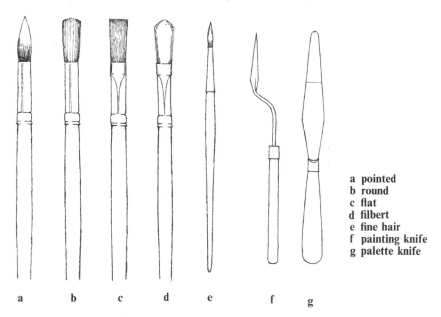

a pointed
b round
c flat
d filbert
e fine hair
f painting knife
g palette knife

a   b   c   d   e   f   g

Fig. 7 brushes and knives

colours, except when used in thin washes, are opaque and cover any surface colour they are painted over. Acrylic or polymer colours may be transparent or opaque depending on whether they are used thinly or thickly. They may be applied as heavy impasto without risk of cracking. All these media may be used to give both delicate and brilliant effects. Decorators' emulsion paint is ideal for covering large areas such as supports for large reliefs. It is possible to mix powder colour into the emulsion to obtain different effects.

Pulped paper made up into reliefs or models may be painted as described above. The surface may be enriched by a coat of polyurethane matt or gloss varnish, applied when the paint is dry.

If you choose an oil-based paint to add a special effect to the work, the paper or support should be sized first, unless it has already been treated in some way to make this unnecessary (e.g. waxed paper or resin-sealed hardboard).

Most papers, except the heaviest quality or waterproof papers, stretch or cockle to varying degrees under a wash of colour unless they are damped and fastened down with gum-strip to a board and allowed to dry out first. As this will often be impracticable in this kind of work, care should be taken not to over-wet the paper and to keep it as flat as possible while the paint is drying.

There are various ways of applying colour:

with a brush
Use the right size for the job: small work needs a small brush, big work a correspondingly big one. Sizes are usually indicated by numbers (0–12 as a rule, and the lower the number, the smaller the brush) or by width (1 in.–4 in. for most purposes). Try also to select the right shape of brush: pointed, round, flat or filbert (tapered) (figs. 7a–d). Brushes made of hair (fig. 7e) are soft and suitable for small work. These are mostly of squirrel, bear, ox, sable or a blend of these. Squirrel is the cheapest, sable the most expensive. Bristle brushes, generally hog bristle, are stiff and good for bigger work. Both kinds may have either

27

short or long handles. Decorators' brushes can be soft or stiff and are useful for covering large areas. Take care of all brushes: do not leave them wet or standing on their bristles.

with a knife
A painting or palette knife (figs. 7f–g) is useful for certain effects. It can be made of metal or plastic, or can be improvised from a piece of thin metal, plastic or wood.

with a diffuser spray (fig. 8a) **or paint aerosol** (fig. 8b)
Useful for colouring work that is difficult to reach with a brush or where a very even or a speckled effect is required. A bristle toothbrush can also be used for spraying colour.

with a natural or foam sponge
Useful for wiping colour on or off and for dabbed and textured effects.

by dipping
Various effects can be obtained by dipping the surface or edge of the paper into a flat trough of water coloured with a paint, ink or dye.

N.B. From now on it will be assumed that the reader will select the best means of applying any paints that are mentioned.

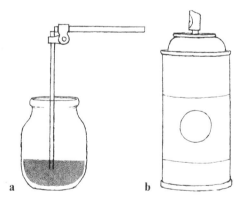

Fig. 8   a   b

Texturing

Adhesive and spreader
Texturing materials: sand; stone, slate or cement dust; fine sawdust;
    flocking; seeds; powdered chalk; other powdered or fine grain
    materials
    At times you may wish to give a textured finish to the surface of the paper or, more likely, to the support. Brush onto the surface an even coating of paste or liquid glue, and sprinkle a suitable material all over it. Shake off any excess when the adhesive is dry. If there are any bare patches, work over them again in the same way. The dried textured surface can be painted or colour-flooded if required.

28

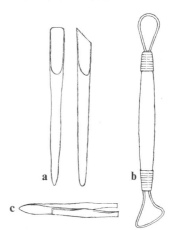

Fig. 9

Modelling

Wooden spatula (fig. 9a)
Wire-ended modelling tool (fig. 9b)
Kitchen knife, fork and spoon
Lollipop stick
Tweezers (fig. 9c)
Home-made tools from scrap, e.g. metal, wood, hard plastic, nails

At least some of these will be needed for modelling with clay (pp. 90, 112), with pulped paper and plaster (pp. 88, 109), or with metal foil (p. 114).

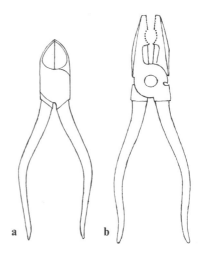

Fig. 10   a   b

Using wire

Brass wire
Copper wire
Florists' wire: in short lengths; a very fine wire
Galvanized wire: probably most useful for wire frameworks
Soft iron wire: in short lengths, bends easily and at angles, useful
   for some construction work
Tinned wire
Wire cutters (fig. 10a)
Pliers (fig. 10b)
Soldering iron and solder

There are several thicknesses (or gauges) of wire, indicated by numbers (the lower the number, the thicker the wire). Some are good for light supports, some for rigid ones, some for bending into flexible shapes. For most work you can join wires by twisting them together. A tinned or copper wire should be used with solder.

Making supports

A support of some kind is needed in all cases where the paper shape is not self-supporting. A support may be flat for work such as collage and reliefs; it may be a means of suspension for work that hangs or moves; it may be three-dimensional for work such as paper structures and models.

The materials and tools needed for mounting a support will be described in some detail here. They will not be listed under the various processes described in later sections of the book unless a special kind of support is needed as in the case of pulped paper reliefs.

a   a flat support
Firm paper, see p. 10
Bristol board: thin, usually white
Corrugated cardboard; in rolls, yellow or grey and some other colours
Manilla: lightweight, smooth, in a range of colours
Millboard: tough, rigid, grey
Pasteboard: smooth, strong, white and coloured
Strawboard: heavy, rigid, straw-coloured
> (The thickness of cardboard is indicated either by weight, or by the number of sheets that make it up, e.g. 3-sheet, 6-sheet. Other useful varieties of cardboard are boxes, cartons, display boards, packing boards.)

Chipboard: made of compressed wood chippings, in large sheets, can be used like wood
Hardboard or Masonite
Insulation or pinboard: this comes in several thicknesses under various trade names (U.K. Sundealer; Celotex); it is softer in texture than hardboard and will take ordinary pins, but it is quite strong and rigid.
Marine plywood: the layers do not warp or peel apart when they are wet
Pegboard: a perforated hardboard
Plywood: 5-ply or 7-ply are most useful
Other timber: fruit boxes; packing cases; tea chests

Most supports have to be cut to the right size and shape to take the work. Scissors or a craft knife will do for the light materials; for others, use a hand or tenon saw or a special cutter designed for the material, e.g. plastic, glass. Smooth any rough edges with sandpaper, glasspaper, or another abrasive.

The support may already have the surface you want for mounting the work on. If not, prepare it in a suitable way:
> paint it (see p. 26)

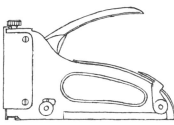

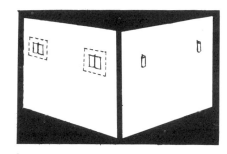

Fig. 11 a   b

texture it (see p. 28)

cover it with another material, e.g. a coloured paper or fabric.

This preparation is important. The support provides the background to the work and may play a part in its final effect. The colour and texture should be right for the work that is being mounted. Is the support to provide a strong contrast or merge with the work? Is it to be opaque or transparent? Are separate areas perhaps to be treated differently, relating them to the arrangement of shapes in the design? The support should be strong enough to prevent it warping when papers are glued to it. Remember that large pieces of paper can set up tensions causing considerable distortion. While the work is drying, keep the support as flat as possible with thumb tacks, staples or with weights of some kind if this can be done without risk to the surface of the design. If the support does warp, reinforce it by fixing it to a firmer one with an adhesive or with staples if they can conveniently be concealed. Framing would also strengthen it.

To mount a flat support for display, use pins, glue or a staple gun (fig. 11a) to fix it to an upright surface. If it is a large sheet of heavier board, wall plugs may be needed to secure it permanently. A useful way to hang a smaller panel of thick card or board is to prepare it for hanging before fixing the work to it. Make two small slits or holes in the support a few inches from the top and an equal distance in from the sides. Ease a loop of tape through them, folding back the two ends and gluing them at the front, leaving just enough of a loop behind to pass the hanging thread through (fig. 11b). Strengthen the turned ends of the tape by gluing a small square of fabric across them.

b   a hanging support

Some work may be designed to hang on a vertical or horizontal support. Attach it to a hanging or stretched thread or fine wire by means of its own parts, a touch of adhesive, a small piece of adhesive tape, or some other suitable method. The paper may need reinforcing at the point of suspension.

c   a three-dimensional support

Some shapes may need a support to help them stand or on which they

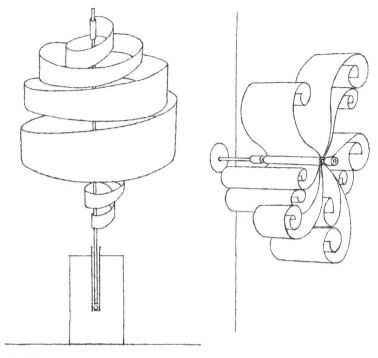

Fig. 12 a   b

can rotate or move. Construct such supports from the lightest rigid materials that will do the job, as a feeling of weight is out of keeping with the lightness of paper. Use rolled or formed paper; cardboard; cane; reed; bamboo; straw stalks; twigs; balsa, match or a similar light wood; dowelling; wire; fine wire mesh; wire wool; expanded polystyrene; plastic; light metal; glass tubes and vessels; scrap and found objects. Secure them by their own parts, an adhesive or adhesive tape, wire, binding thread, pins or other suitable means. Design the support to be concealed or to play an integral part in the finished work.

For some of the modelled work with layered or pulped paper, you will want a sturdier support, e.g. metal; wood; heavier scrap.

At times you may need a specially-shaped support, e.g. a dished or bowl form; a ball; a box; a paper, cardboard or plastic carton; a polythene dispenser; a made-up form of some other kind.

A turning support can be of any suitable length material, e.g. a fine wire rod or dowelling. The turning end should be smooth and housed in a sleeve secured to hold the shape upright or to project it at the required angle (fig. 12a). A little grease or French chalk will help lubricate it. If the shape is designed to turn on a fixed support, it should be assembled around a sleeve on the support with a stop at either end of the sleeve to prevent it sliding along, (fig. 12b). The sleeve may be of rolled paper, hard plastic tubing or something equally simple, and can be incorporated as part of the overall shape.

Paint or texture the support if needed (see pp. 26–28).

Other materials

Strictly speaking, papercraft is carried out with paper. There are, however, many materials which have qualities similar to paper, or which associate naturally with it. There may be opportunities for using some of these in your work, discovering ways in which they can extend and enrich it. Such materials might include light fabrics—lace, cotton net, gauze, silk, organdie, muslin, cheesecloth, stocking mesh, nylon net, synthetic fibres; light card and corrugated cardboard; dried reeds, grass, ferns, seeds and other plant forms; feathers; dress accessories such as sequins and beads; film; thin plastics; wood veneers and shavings; spills (wood splinters); matchbox wood; packing straw; expanded polystyrene; drinking straws; thread and twine; fine wire; other light scrap.

4 Using paper flat

Before starting on any of the processes described in this book, check the list of materials and tools you will need. These are set out at the beginning of each process, with alternative or optional ones in brackets. The reader should refer back to Part 3 for any further information about them.

Unless a paper shape is designed to stand by itself, it will need a support of some kind. The support can be flat, hanging or three-dimensional (see pp. 30–33).

Torn and cut shapes

Any variety of paper
Scissors, craft knife and cutting board
Adhesive, spreader
Support and materials
(Drawing medium; paint; ink)

a from single sheets

i Tearing shapes from paper is rather like making an outline drawing. The shapes can be torn freely to give a lively edge or with more care to give an accurate one (p. 12). You can tear a shape direct from the paper, being guided largely by the way in which the paper behaves (often the best way), or you can make a light drawing on the paper as a guide.

If shapes are torn from very thin paper, you will probably want to fix them afterwards to a firmer support with adhesive or pins (p. 30). A design may be built up from any number of shapes and completed if necessary with paint or ink.

If shapes are torn from thicker paper, you may:
complete a design as above
stand the shapes by curving or folding the paper to stay upright, or by bending back part of the shape as a foot
support them from behind (p. 30)
suspend them from a vertical or horizontal thread (p. 31)

Combining any of these methods it is possible to devise interesting situations with a variety of shapes, e.g. airborne shapes suspended over others on the ground. Two or more shapes can be joined together by adhesive or other means.

Paper shapes are often best left as they are, but detail may be drawn or painted onto them as desired. Keep the paper weighted in some way to prevent it from curling.

In fig. 13 white thread was stretched across an old picture frame. The shapes of clouds, scarecrow and landscape were torn from wallpaper, tissue and wrapping papers, held in place between the threads with a touch of glue here and there.

ii Shapes that are cut out have a different character from those that are torn: the outlines are sharper and the details crisper. It is also possible to achieve finer detail within the shape. Use scissors or a craft

Fig. 13

knife, whichever seems right for the paper and the job you are doing.

The birds and balloon (fig. 14) were cut from drawing paper and suspended by threads. The church was made from a thin cardboard box and corrugated paper. All cutting was done with a craft knife.

iii Cut shapes can be raised to stand away from a single sheet of paper. Lay the paper flat and cut shapes from it with a craft knife, leaving one side of each shape uncut. Raise the cut-away part, creasing along the uncut side to make the shape stand at the required angle. Shapes may either be cut freely as the work progresses, or may be planned and drawn out lightly first. Light and shadow will create its own interest, and different coloured papers behind the openings will add a further contrast. Shapes cut away from the edges of the paper can be folded back onto a contrasting background, and can be pasted down to lie flat.

The animal and grasses (fig. 15) were cut from a single sheet of thick typing paper and raised to leave the cut-away parts as 'shadows' on a

Fig. 14
Fig. 15
Fig. 16

Fig. 17

dark paper underneath. Similarly the crab and waves (fig. 16) were formed by cutting into a sheet of paper and raising the shapes.

b   from folded sheets
i   By folding the paper over on itself a number of times and cutting a shape from it, you unfold the same number of shapes as there are layers of the paper. If you want joined shapes, leave at least part of each folded edge uncut. Because they open out at an angle to each other, joined shapes of any thickish paper will stand by themselves.

The Druids and stone circle (fig. 17) were cut with scissors from folded typing and drawing paper.
ii   It is always a surprise to see how paper multiplies and transforms a few simple cuts made when it is folded over in different ways. The most intricate designs may appear when the paper is opened out. However the paper was cut and folded, something of interest will have happened. The paper may be folded and re-folded at right angles to itself or diagonally, forming pleats, darts and other kinds of shapes. A few experiments cutting away small parts of this shape will soon show the changes that take place. Use fairly thin paper otherwise it will become too thick to cut when folded. Cut away only small areas at first, or there may not be much left when the paper is opened out. Now and again the paper may come away in more than one piece; but this is all part of finding out what the cutting does. Early attempts can be simply experi-

Fig. 18 a   c
               b   d

mental: later the different effects may be planned more deliberately.

These designs are set off well when pasted to a support (p. 30). A number of them may be combined on one support and linked into a more complex design, perhaps with each one backed with a different colour (see also pp. 106, 108). They may also be used in other paper crafts such as flower making and collage (p. 41) or mounted and made up as greeting cards, table place mats or decoration for a party.

Thin typing paper was used for the examples of folded cuts (fig. 18). For designs a and b the paper was folded in half a number of times; for c and d it was folded over in strips. They were all cut with small nail scissors.

iii Cut a length of paper and make it up into a roll-over or zig-zag fold. Make cuts at intervals all along one side up to a centre line: the cuts can be at any angle to the side but should be parallel. Make similar cuts from the other side so that they end in between the first ones. Unroll the paper and raise alternate shapes between the cuts. Emphasize the creases to bring these out more clearly. As above the effect can be heightened by lighting or a coloured backing.

Fig. 19a

b

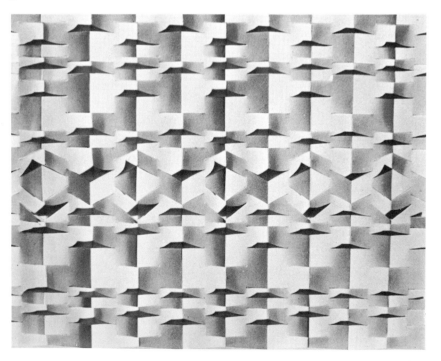

40

Lengths of paper cut like this can be made up into standing forms, either rounded or square-sided.

The folded cut (fig. 19) shows a single design photographed with light directed from different sides.

Collage

Assortment of papers
Scissors (craft knife and cutting board)
Adhesive, spreader: for most work cellulose paste and a decorator's
  brush 1–2 in. wide will be suitable, although certain papers may
  want a stronger adhesive and a different kind of spreader.
Support and materials
(Painting or drawing media: texturing materials)

A collage is made by sticking torn or cut paper shapes to a flat support to make a design. Effects of great subtlety or richness can be discovered by using the various papers in different ways both for their own abstract qualities and for interpreting other subjects. The right combination or overlaying of papers can create almost any kind of surface: misty, melting, vibrating, glowing, fragmented, eruptive, flowing, rhythmic, still. They can express a particular mood or feeling or represent anything one sees or imagines.

First select the papers. Should they be flimsy and transparent or firm and thick? Should they be coloured, plain, patterned, smooth or textured? Will they change at all when pasted and stuck down (p. 9)?
i When making a design of the paper shapes for their own sake, a good way to start is to scatter a variety of papers loose on a table and move them about together to see what effects they have on each other. Even one kind of paper alone can have an exciting range of tones and colours. Tear out a few biggish pieces (tearing is usually better than cutting as the results are more interesting), and arrange them in different ways on a flat surface to meet or overlap. Try them out in various positions before deciding finally where the main shapes will be. Transfer and stick down the main pieces to a support (p. 30), pasting either the support or the pieces, whichever is easier. (In the case of tissues, for example, the support will almost certainly have to be pasted as they are unmanageable wet.) Paste may be brushed *over* the pieces to work them flat: a cellulose paste will dry out without leaving marks (see note on polyurethane varnish, p. 9). Tear and paste down further pieces, letting the design develop gradually. There is no need to wait for earlier layers to dry before adding new ones. Remember that, at every stage, the shapes into which the paper tears naturally can suggest further ideas: some interesting developments come from this.

For a more direct approach, prepare a support first and start straight away tearing and pasting shapes of paper to it, letting each addition suggest what the next should be. The difference here is that you are working within a set area and being guided to a greater extent by the shapes the paper takes up.

Fig. 20   Fig. 21

ii If you want to build up a particular picture, tear or cut out the shapes and arrange them on a table or board; then, being careful to start with any underneath ones first, transfer and paste them to the support. Any preparatory drawing on the support should be only enough to help position the main pieces. The quicker it is covered up the better for, in trying to keep too closely to it, shapes will lose much of their spontaneity and any chance suggestion that the paper could have given will be missed.

Keep all completed work as flat as possible while it is drying by pinning it to a firm surface or by weighting it down if this can be managed without risk to the pasted parts.

The landscape with flowers (fig. 20) was made from magazine advertisements and wallpaper. The owl (fig. 21) was made up of folded cuts (p. 38), the tree from parts of a cosmetics gift box and strips of cellophane, the background from carbon and wrapping paper and glitter. The pieces were stuck onto thin card.

A paper collage sometimes provides a good foundation for painting, and you can work onto it with paint or texture if you see the possibilities. You can paint water or emulsion colour straight onto the paper: with oils, size the collage first to ensure that the paint does not dry into it and become dull.

Fig. 22

44

Fig. 23

Montage

Old magazines (newspapers; periodicals; discarded personal
  photographs; posters; reproduced pictures from other sources)
Scissors (craft knife and cutting board)
Adhesive, spreader: cellulose paste and a paste brush will be suitable
  for most work
Support and materials

Montage is the pasting of cut-out photographs and other kinds of illustration to a plain background or another picture to produce a new effect. The intention can be serious or lighthearted. The choice and arrangement of the cut-outs can suggest impossible situations, fantasies, dramatic or comic incident—almost any subject you care to invent. A bundle of old magazines or newspapers or discarded personal photographs should provide all necessary material. Cut out from various pictures a few figures, animals, buildings, pieces of machinery, vehicles and other items and arrange them in different ways alongside or on top of each other until an idea comes. Hunt out any further pictures needed to complete the idea, and then paste them all down to the support. If one cut-out it to be on top of another, be sure to paste the underneath one down first.

If, instead, you paste cut-outs onto another picture, you can change its appearance or significance by what you add (see fig. 22).

Counter-change

2 (or 3) sheets of different coloured paper
Craft knife and cutting board
Adhesive, spreader

A counter-change is made by arranging a number of shapes to correspond with similar ones of a contrasting colour opposite them so that one side seems to reflect the other. Only two different coloured sheets of paper are required, e.g. black and white, blue and grey, one of them exactly half the size of the other.

With a craft knife, cut away cleanly a few interesting shapes from the smaller piece. Place what is left of this piece over one half of the larger paper which will then show through the cut-away parts. Arrange the cut-away shapes themselves on the other half directly opposite the holes they have left, as they would be if they mirrored them. Notice the effect this is producing, then cut away and arrange any further shapes to complete it. Stick all the pieces in place on the larger sheet of paper. The lighthouse (fig. 23) was made up of shapes cut from a smaller sheet of white paper and pasted down on the black.

It is possible to make a counter-change using three colours of paper. One piece is used as the background. Lay the other two pieces together and cut out a variety of shapes from them simultaneously so that there are two sets of corresponding shapes, each a different colour. Arrange and paste these down opposite each other on the background sheet. Alterna-

Fig. 24 a

b

tively, paste down what is left of the two pieces of paper with their shapes removed.

Silhouettes

A sheet of white or coloured paper
Scissors (craft knife and cutting board)
Adhesive, spreader
Drawing medium
Support and materials

A silhouette is an arrangement of shapes cut from one colour of paper and pasted to a contrasting background. The effect can be bold and simple, or quite intricate and detailed.

Lightly draw the shape of the silhouette on the paper. Using small pointed scissors or a craft knife cut away any details *within* the main outline; this will leave the rest of the paper acting as a support while you are doing it. Then cut round the outlines to detach the main shape.

Prepare a background for mounting it. Paper would be suitable, but a firmer surface may be selected instead (p. 30). It could be of one or more colours, or even be designed as a setting for the silhouette; but the silhouette should stand out clearly against it. Paste the silhouette to it, keeping it flat while it is drying.

The first harvest scene (fig. 24a) was cut from black construction paper with a craft knife and pasted onto white: the second (24b) shows the surrounding black paper pasted onto white, creating a different silhouette effect.

Mosaics

White or coloured paper (see below)
Scissors (craft knife and cutting board)
Adhesive, spreader
Drawing medium
Support and materials

A mosaic is made by fixing lots of small squarish pieces of material close together to a firm surface to make a design. They can be touching or a little apart. These pieces would normally be of some hard material like glass, marble or fired clay. Because paper is thin and light it does not suffer from the limitations of those materials and could be allowed to overlap in any variety of shapes. Nevertheless, the effects of combining small squares of paper can have an appeal all of its own. As only regular-shaped pieces are used for a mosaic, the process might suggest a fairly formal treatment of subjects; but you can also achieve very lively effects of movement and massing with it. Tones can be shaded off subtly into each other; areas of colour can be made to vibrate with countless small variations within them; quite fine detail can be worked out with very small pieces. Mosaic should not aim at what a painting

Fig. 25 a   b

could do better, but develop a design through its own characteristic shapes.

To cut out lots of squares at once, fold over several thicknesses of paper and cut them into strips of one width. Lay the strips on top of each other and cut off similar widths all the way along them. Do the same with strips of other widths to make different sized squares. It helps to keep all these in separate containers so that the different sizes can be selected easily.

Prepare a support (p. 30). It should be a different colour from most of the squares. Sketch out the main shapes of the design on the support, then arrange the squares and paste them into place. The sketch can only be a broad guide: the direction and grouping of the squares may change it from time to time in keeping with their own nature. Do not try and force them to do unnatural things or attempt more detail than their size allows: used *as* squares, they can lead to more fitting solutions than could otherwise have been found. You may prefer to build up the mosaic directly onto the support without any guide lines; it could develop more freely in this way.

a   using squares of one colour

This kind of mosaic relies entirely on the arrangement and grouping of

48

the pieces for its effect, as colour changes play no part in it. Decide on different sizes of squares to define the various parts of the design—one size to lead the eye along lines, increasing or decreasing as the line broadens or narrows; matching sizes grouped to distinguish one area from another; tightly packed squares to give a different character from areas where they are more widely spaced. With a little planning, the squares can be organized into patterns of movement and rest, giving a feeling of their own or representing some other subject.

Different sized squares were cut from drawing paper to make the fire mosaic (fig. 25a). Paste was spread on black card in small areas at a time and the squares slid into position with tweezers.

b using different coloured squares
All sorts of coloured paper can be used, including old magazines, wall and wrapping paper. Decide on the colour or texture for each part of the design, arranging for them to merge or contrast as you wish. Colours from one part of the spectrum can often be grouped together to make a richer or more subtle effect, e.g. blues and greens to give an iridescent turquoise, or red with yellows and orange mixed with it to make it more fiery. Remember that the mosaic will be viewed from a short distance away, allowing the colours to blend together. The viewing distance should be kept in mind throughout: different areas may stand out better than they seem to at close quarters.

The squares for the sea wall mosaic (fig. 25b) were cut from a glossy magazine advertisement, and put together as above. Two different backing colours were used.

See-through shapes

Sheet of firm paper
Craft knife and cutting board (scissors)
Adhesive, spreader
Drawing medium
Paint (ink)
Support and materials
A design can be cut away from paper, and the resulting shape set up against a source of light or against a backing that can be seen through it.

Although the paper acts mainly as a silhouette, its surface is still seen and is therefore as much a part of it as the shapes that are cut away, especially if it is to stand against a background colour rather than against the light. The effect lies in the contrast between the shapes that are removed and the tracery they leave. The tracery would appear dark against a source of light and could appear either dark or light against a coloured backing.

Several possible ways of setting up your work are listed below. Plan with them in mind. Use a reasonably firm opaque paper and lightly draw out the shapes of the parts to be removed. Lay the paper on a board and cut the parts away with a sharp craft knife, starting with the smallest

D

Fig. 26

ones and turning the paper whenever necessary to make the work easier. Be careful not to cut into the tracery between the shapes: if this happens by accident, a small piece of thin paper pasted behind the cut will hold it together and probably not be noticeable. Carefully erase any marks left by the pencil and set up your work in any of the following ways:

i Design and cut the paper to stand without support as a folding screen.
ii Design and cut the paper to stand as a cylinder. Glue the two meeting edges, and the bottom edge if it is to be fixed to a base. A roll of another coloured paper or gelatine inside the cylinder (perhaps containing a light) will lend a different effect.
iii Design and cut the paper as a curved screen. Cut a piece of cardboard to the correct shape for the base. Lightly glue the under edge of the paper screen and fix it into place on the cardboard, holding it while the glue sets. A vertical strip of balsa wood or a similar material glued down the sides will reinforce it if necessary.
iv If the paper is firm enough, glue it to a right-angled or wedge-shaped

piece of cardboard at the back, or to a simple framework of rigid wire, balsa wood or cardboard strips braced to stand or fixed into a base.

v   Glue or staple the paper flat into a light, standing frame.

vi Suspend the paper by fine thread, strengthening edges where necessary with rigid wire, narrow strips of cardboard or balsa wood.

vii Fix the paper upright to a standing, coloured backing of a rigid material by means of connecting lengths of balsa wood, dowelling or cardboard. It could be fixed close to the backing or some distance away from it.

viii Cut out two opposite sides of a box and glue the paper across one side. Alternatively, cut out one side of the box only and wire a lamp inside to throw the paper into silhouette.

ix Paste the paper directly onto a rigid coloured backing, or to a sheet of glass so as to form a tracery design when placed against the light.

The windows and the shapes seen through them in 'Evening at Home' (fig. 26) were all cut with a craft knife from one sheet of dark construction paper. The curtains are strips of tissue. The top of a gift box lid was cut away, and the paper glued in its place.

Transparent shapes

Transparent papers
Scissors (craft knife and cutting board)
Adhesive, spreader
Support and materials

The overlapping or combining of different varieties of transparent paper can produce both rich and subtle depths of colour. Of the papers which are virtually transparent when placed against a light, perhaps the most useful here are clear and coloured tissues, cellophane, rice paper, tracing and greaseproof paper, and some of the cellulose papers. Small pieces such as confectionery wrappers have as much value as larger pieces.

Paste different shapes of contrasting paper to each other to build up a design of their overlapping areas. Trim the edges of the design to shape and set it up by any of the appropriate methods listed in the previous section. Alternatively you could overlap only the edges of the pieces making a design of single areas of colour. Be prepared for the paper to cockle when pasted: pressed out, this can produce some interesting surface texture. Paper pasted directly onto glass or firm gelatine and plastic sheets can be smoothed out quite flat. Torn tissues were pasted to a sheet of glass to make the hills (fig. 27).

Another variation is to make up a number of flat, transparent shapes supported by a light framework of wire, balsa wood or cardboard. They might be set at short intervals apart and at different heights one behind the other. Seen from one end and against the light, the overlapping planes will set up various depths of colour.

Coloured transparent papers also make a good backing for a see-through shape (p. 49). Paste them to the reverse side, stopping every so

Fig. 27

Fig. 28

often to see the effect when the shape is held against the light.

Projection slides

Thin glass
Glass cutter
Straight edge
Cellophane (clear candy wrappers; gelatines)
Scissors (craft knife and cutting board)
Cellulose tape
Slide projector
(Adhesive—a dot glue pen is useful; thread or wire)

The projection of light through coloured transparent papers can create an endless variety of brilliant effects. Some lovely designs come almost by accident, but with experience you can plan for a particular image.

Cut two squares of thin glass to fit into a slide projector, e.g. 2 in. × 2 in. Cut some small shapes of coloured cellophane or gelatine, and arrange them on one of the squares so that they overlap (fig. 28). Lay the other square on top and, keeping the two squares pressed together, hinge or bind round the edges with clear cellulose tape to complete the slide. This will project on the screen as a colour image which can easily be varied by changing the position of the pieces. If the pieces are to be fixed in position, use a bead of clear adhesive here and there before sealing them between the glass squares: the glue spots themselves will appear as dark areas in the design, and this should be taken into consideration. Dark lines can be introduced into the design with fine thread or florists' wire: the pressure of the glass should keep them in place.

Prints with paper

Sheet of good quality cartridge or drawing paper (another strong
    paper; vinyl wallpaper; doilies; glossy magazine paper)
Scissors (craft knife and cutting board)
Adhesive—preferably gum or glue; spreader
Cardboard (pinboard; hardboard; formica)
Linoleum printing ink—preferably oil-based
Inking plate: glazed tile (piece of formica or hard plastic; zinc or
    other metal plate; piece of cork linoleum; hardboard or Masonite
    sealed with primer, emulsion or house paint; plate glass; ordinary
    glass)
Roller(s)
Printing paper: some of the lightweight and slightly stronger papers,
    e.g. detail and thin typing paper
Thumb tacks
Flat iron
(Burnishing tool)

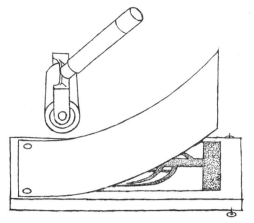

Fig. 29

a a raised paper print

Torn or cut paper shapes can be reproduced as a print. The flat or textured areas and the ragged or clean edges combine to give all kinds of print effects.

i Use a stout paper: it should be smooth, like heavy drawing paper, or smoothly textured like some of the thicker vinyl wallpapers (printing from thinner papers could be disappointing at first). Tear or cut out a few simple shapes to make a design—the simpler the better: they will print more clearly than complicated ones. The shapes should overlap as little as possible since overlapping raises the level of the paper in places and makes inking uneven, although with practice you may be able to produce this effect intentionally as part of the design.

Cut a piece of cardboard or similar flat material the size of your design, and stick down the shapes of paper firmly with gum or glue. When this is completely dry, it is ready for printing. Lay it face up on a piece of newspaper. Put out some printing ink on a flat plate and roll out the ink evenly with a print roller. Roll the ink over the surface of the design, making sure all parts are covered. Lay a sheet of printing paper carefully onto the inked design, pinning it at one end if necessary to keep it from moving, and work over it in all directions with a clean roller or a smooth burnishing tool such as a spoon handle. Lift one end of the paper. If the print is not clear, replace the paper and work over it again. The print may have picked up some ink from between the shapes, especially if the paper shapes were rather thin; but this can often be an attractive feature of the print. The number of prints that can be taken is limited, as the paper surface tends to pull away after a time.

ii Prepare a design from paper shapes and stick it down to a support as above. When it is dry, lay it face up on a board and pin a larger sheet of printing paper to lie over it. Ink up the roller very lightly and evenly. Take off any surplus ink on some scrap paper: over-inking of the roller will make marks on the printing paper where they are not wanted. Work gently over the paper with the charged roller (fig. 29) until a clear impression of the design comes through. Accidental texturing of the paper around the shapes, as long as it is only light, can create interesting tone effects. After a certain amount of experiment you will be able to design a print with these effects in mind.

To make the print of an old tree (fig. 30) the trunk and branches were cut from thick drawing paper and glued to a board. A print was then taken as above.

Fig. 30

Fig. 31   Fig. 32

b   a masked print
In this method of printing, the paper is used to mask off certain areas
and create negative shapes on the colour.
i   Select a suitable inking plate (see above). Tear or cut out a few simple
shapes from *thin* paper to make a design that fits the plate, and lay the
pieces to one side for a moment. Ink up the plate evenly all over with a
roller and transfer the design of paper shapes to it, pressing each piece
down gently so that it adheres to the ink. Lay a sheet of printing paper
over the plate and press it out under a clean roller: only the unmasked
areas of colour will print. The design of rose and thorns (fig. 31) was
made in this way.
ii   Tear or cut out shapes from a sheet of *thin* paper and lay what is
left of the sheet on an inked plate; then lay printing paper over it and
press out as above.
iii   Using the torn or cut edge of a piece of paper to mask part of the
printing paper, ink a roller and roll the colour along it: the mark of the
roller will be masked by the edge of the paper. Move the piece of paper
to cover another part of the printing paper and repeat the process,
building up a design from the resulting edges. This method was used
for the print of the sea (fig. 32). When the waves had been printed, they
were masked completely and ink was rolled up the paper to indicate the
sky.

c   a crumpled paper print
Crumple a sheet of strong cartridge or heavy drawing paper with varying

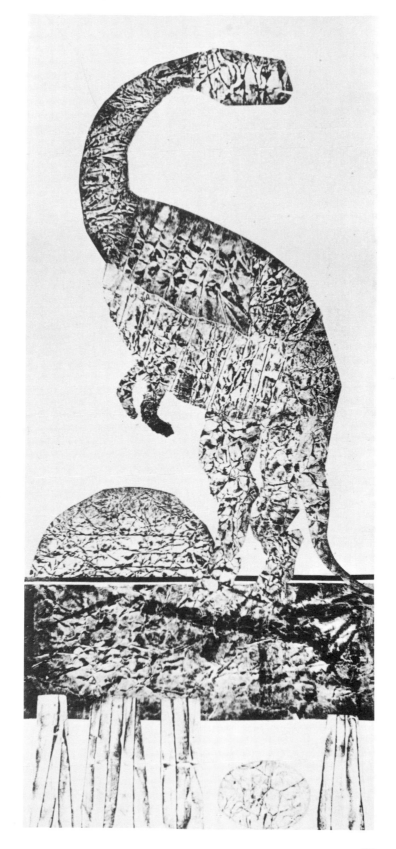

Fig. 33

Fig. 34   Fig. 35

pressures to produce both deep and shallow creasing. Flatten it out on a piece of scrap paper. Ink a roller and roll it across the ridges of the crumpled paper in all directions, making a 'crackle' design. Re-ink, and work over again any areas where you want a darker tone. With experience, you will be able to crumple and ink the paper with greater control and achieve a planned effect. When the ink is dry, iron out the paper under a sheet of scrap paper.

As a further experiment shapes may be cut or torn from a number of different prints and reassembled on a support as a collage. There is no need to iron them flat before gluing them down. The dinosaur guarding her egg (fig. 33) was made in this way.

d   a positive and negative print
Cut out a design of shapes from a sheet of thin paper. Lay the shapes on
another sheet of paper, temporarily securing them with a touch of
flexible adhesive such as Copydex. (The shapes will be lifted off later,
so must come away easily.) Ink the roller well, and roll it evenly across
the shapes and the sheet to which they are glued. Make sure that all the
shapes and the exposed parts of the underlying sheet are covered. Lift
off the cut-out shapes: they will leave a corresponding negative design
on the paper underneath. By experimenting with different arrangements
of these two sets of shapes, and perhaps by cutting here and there, you
will be able to bring out their full contrasting effect. Finally glue down the
cut-out shapes on the negative design. The cranes in the industrial scene
(fig. 34) were built up in this way.

e   a twisted paper print
Make a small pad of absorbent cloth or soft foam plastic and put it in
a saucer. Add enough ink or powder colour and paste mixture to soak
the pad.
Twist up a small piece of paper and press it lightly into the pad. Press
the inked shape onto a sheet of paper, developing a design from the
mark it makes. Turn the shape this way and that, re-inking it from time
to time as necessary. Print heavily or lightly, or overprint to obtain more
dense effects. You may find you have to twist up a new shape if the first
one becomes flattened or if you need a different kind of mark. Three
different twists of paper were used to print the frog, the spawn and
the floating weeds (fig. 35).

Sandwich designs

1 or 2 sheets of cartridge paper (heavy drawing paper; a similar paper)
Thread
Ink (paint)
Board
Matchstick (drinking straw; twig; feather)
(Pen; brush)
The sandwich is made up of two sheets of cartridge or similar quality
paper with a 'filling' squeezed between them to make a design.

a   thread
i   Soak a length of thread in ink and, while it is still wet, let it fall
freely on a sheet of paper with one or both of the ends of thread hanging
an inch or so over the near edge of the paper. Lay another sheet of
paper on top of the first. Hold the sandwiched papers flat under a board
and draw out the thread, moving it from side to side. This will produce
a line and tone 'drawing' on both pieces of paper. You may add to the
design of marks by re-inking the thread, perhaps in another colour,
or by working from another edge of the paper, and repeating the
process. All kinds of flowing, intricate and subtle designs can result. The

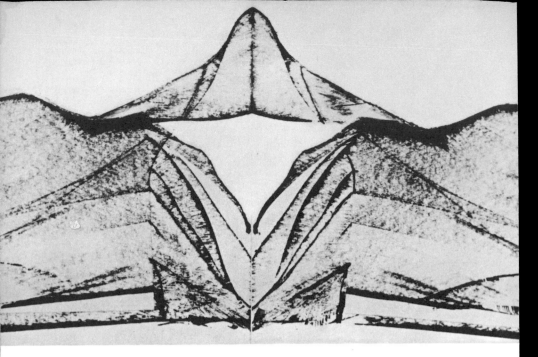

Fig. 36 a

b

mountain landscape (fig. 36a) is an example of this.

ii Let inked thread fall freely onto a sheet of paper (without hanging the ends over the edge this time) and lay a second sheet on it. Just press them out under a board or with a clean roller to produce a line 'drawing' on each. If, instead of two separate sheets, you use one folded sheet with inked thread on just one half, a mirrored 'drawing' will result.

b ink

Fold a sheet of cartridge or drawing paper in half and open it out flat on a table. Let a few drops of ink or paint fall on one half up to the crease and fold the halves over, pressing them out under the flat of the hands. This will produce a mirror design on the opened sheet. See what this suggests, and add further drops on one half to develop the idea, moving them about quickly with the end of a matchstick before the ink dries. Fold and press the halves together and see how the idea has grown. It may be best to use only light pressure on the paper so as to avoid spreading the colour too far or blurring any line effects. Continue adding small drops of ink or paint and drawing through them, folding and pressing out the paper each time. Remember to work on one half only: it will be reproduced exactly on the other.

With pen or brush drawing you may develop the resulting image still further. This may even give ideas for further paintings.

The girls and dogs (fig. 36b) were developed by drawing with a matchstick into a few blots of ink.

Weaving

Two or more kinds of contrasting paper
Scissors (craft knife and cutting board)
Adhesive, spreader
Cardboard
(Straight edge)

Strips of paper can be woven in much the same way as yarn or fabric strips. You may not have to look further than a pile of old papers or ends of wallpaper rolls for all the material you need. Full page illustrations from supplements and similar magazines can be cut into interesting strips: the colour and tone changes give a rich effect in the finished work (fig. 37). Even pages of print give a tone contrast when they are woven with white or coloured paper.

Use two contrasting papers, e.g. plain and coloured, light and dark, smooth and textured. Cut both papers into strips of similar or different widths, keeping each set separate. One of these will be the warp (up and down), the other the weft (from side to side).

i Cut a rectangle of card a little shorter than the warp lengths and a little narrower than the weft lengths. Paste the end of the warp strips along the reverse top edge of the card, and bend them over forward to lie flat side by side down the front. They can be close together or spaced a little apart.

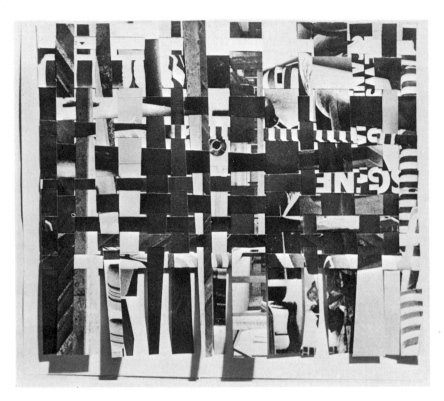

Fig. 37

Working with the other set of strips (the weft), pass the first strip under and over the warp strips, leaving a short length at either end for tucking behind the card later. Ease the strip well up to the top of the warp. Pass the second one under and over alternate warp strips, leaving a short length either end as before and easing the strip up to the first one. Continue in this way with the rest of the weft, choosing the most suitable strips from the set to build up the weaving pattern. When it is complete, paste the loose ends of the warp strips to the reverse side of the card, and do the same with the ends of the weft strips, taking up any slack. The edges should now be neat and secure.

ii Weave the paper strips without a card support. Prepare the two sets as before, then pin the ends of one set (the warp) to a board and weave the other strips through them, letting them jut out a little at start and finish. Unpin them and, keeping the weaves in place, trim and fold back all the ends alternate ways. Secure them with a touch of adhesive.

Another alternative would be to glue the top ends of the warp to a strip of paper and pin this strip to a board to hold it in place while you weave.

iii Yet another, and perhaps simpler, approach is to use a sheet of paper as the warp. Rule lines horizontally across the paper equal distances apart (the ruled page of an exercise book may do). Rule a line vertically down each side, a little way in from the edges. With a craft knife, cut along the horizontal lines, starting and finishing the cuts at the vertical lines. The parallel strips between the cuts become the warp.

Cut strips of contrasting paper, and weave them in and out of the warp strips, keeping them very close together. Secure them top and bottom with a touch of adhesive.

By making staggered slits in the warp sheet the same width as the weft strips and just overlapping each other, you will be able to devise other kinds of woven design.

Stencils

A sheet of good cartridge paper (construction paper; manilla; waxed
    paper; oiled paper; vinyl paper)
Craft knife or stencil knife and cutting board
Drawing medium
Pins (thumb tacks; cellulose tape)
Powder colour (poster paint; household emulsion; acrylic paint; oil
    paint; ink; dye)
Stencilling brush (short bristle paint brush; foam or natural sponge;
    twist of fabric or paper; bottle cork)
Material on which to stencil: paper (cardboard; pinboard; hardboard;
    fabric; planed wood; tile)

You can make a design by cutting shapes away from a firm piece of paper and dabbing colour through the holes to reproduce the shapes on another surface: only the exposed parts of this surface receive the colour. The effect can vary with the way the colour is applied. Solid areas of colour are produced by working over all exposed parts with equal pressure; toned areas of colour when unequal pressure is used; colour-edged areas when only the edges of the holes are treated. Mixed effects are achieved by changing the colour.

The best results usually come from simple cutting, though more complex shapes can be cut and, with the correct consistency of paint, stencilled successfully onto the surface beneath. Use a fairly stout paper for the stencil, e.g. good cartridge, construction or manilla paper—or, better still, a damp-resistant waxed, oiled or vinyl paper. Draw on the stencilling paper the shapes you are going to remove and lay the paper flat on a board to cut them away. Be careful not to cut into the supporting paper between the shapes or to make the supports too narrow as the colour will spread beneath them. Pin or tape the stencil flat over the material to be stencilled. Make up a fairly stiff mixture of paint and apply it with gentle dabbing movement. If the paint is worked from side to side it will spread under the masked parts of the stencil and spoil the sharpness of the design. Experiment with a number of ready-made brushes or improvised tools to discover the different effects they give.

Fig. 38

'Apparition' (fig. 38) was stencilled with a small wad of net curtain. Wait for the paint to dry, then lift off the stencil. Ink or dye may be used instead of paint, but these are thin and more likely to run under the stencil unless used sparingly and with care. They can, however, produce both brilliant and soft effects.

Dip-dye designs

Paper towel (similar absorbent paper)
Cold or hot water dye
Flat dish
    The characteristic of highly absorbent papers like paper towels to take

up water makes it possible to create simple dye patterns with them.

Mix the dye and pour some in a flat dish. Fold a paper towel length-wise several times like a screen. Hold it, edge down, and surface-dip it in the dye. The dye will be drawn up into the paper a certain distance by capillary action (fig. 39) and will show a repeating pattern when the paper is unfolded.

As a further experiment, you could re-fold the dipped paper at right angles to the first folds and re-dip it. Interesting effects will come from using a second colour or from folding the paper in different ways.

The patterns can be cut up and re-assembled to make a collage.

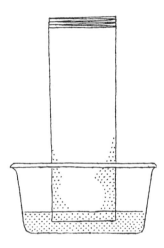

Fig. 39

5 Using paper in relief

The relief effect depends on the contrast between the raised paper shapes, the support on which they are mounted, and the movement of light and shadow over them. The part light plays is important, as a great variety of changes can be produced by directing it on the work from different angles, and by using different coloured lights. You should bear this in mind while constructing the relief.

A fairly stiff paper is needed for most of the following processes, together with a support (p. 30).

Crumpled

Any paper
Scissors
Adhesive, spreader: paste is suitable for most jobs
Support and materials
(Paint; texture materials; ink and diffuser; paint aerosol)

Fig. 40   **Fig. 41**

a firm paper

When you crumple a sheet of a paper and flatten it out a little, it will have irregular contours rather like a landscape. The effect varies with the thickness of the paper and the amount it is pressed and flattened out: one result could be only slightly uneven, another rugged and precipitous. Colour and texture also play a part in the effect. These qualities of different papers can be set off against each other to make a relief.

Select a few papers of different thickness, colour or texture. Crumple them *with varying pressures*. Straighten them out and lay them together in different arrangements, letting them over-ride each other wherever you think fit, so that a continuous area of changing relief and surface is set up. The change can be gradual or clearly defined, depending on the effect you want and the qualities of the juxtaposed papers. Trim any edges that are to fit closely.

Prepare a support to the shape of the final arrangement, and colour or texture any areas that are to remain showing between the paper. Paste the support and transfer the paper to it, pressing pieces down very gently in order not to flatten the raised parts, and holding them in place until they are stuck. Be careful to lay any underneath ones down first. If both upper and underneath pieces are to be on the same level, flatten the underneath piece where the other one is to lie and spread paste on the flattened part. If the upper piece is to ride on top of the other, spread paste on its underside before lowering it into position.

You can accentuate the relief by spraying at a fairly low angle from one side only. Use a diffuser with ink or a paint aerosol, but do not make the paper too wet.

Alternatively, you can prepare a support and build up the design to fit it. A selection of pastel, typing and drawing papers was used to make up the relief of a glacier (fig. 40).

b soft paper

Some thin papers such as tissue paper will crumple tightly and can be used to build areas of quite dense texture. The support may be pasted as above and the modelled forms pressed onto it; or the paper may be soaked in paste and modelled wet onto the support. As the colour in many of these papers is not fast, you should be prepared for it to spread. This can be quite effective.

The fossil skeleton (fig. 41) is modelled with coloured tissues and carbon paper onto hardboard (Masonite).

Folded, rolled and curved

Any fairly firm paper
Scissors (craft knife and cutting board)
Adhesive, spreader: tube glue is suitable
Bone folder (similar folding tool)
Straight edge   Pencil
Support and materials

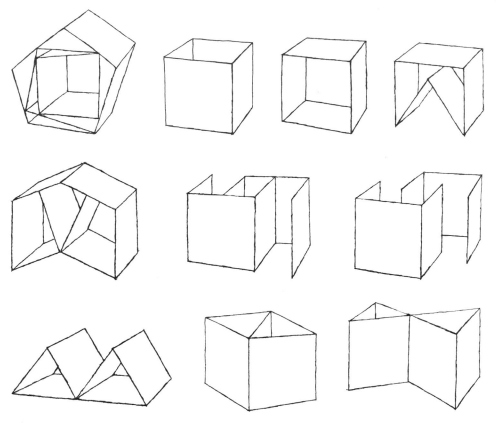

Fig. 42 variations on a roll-over fold

Fig. 43 variations on a zig-zag fold

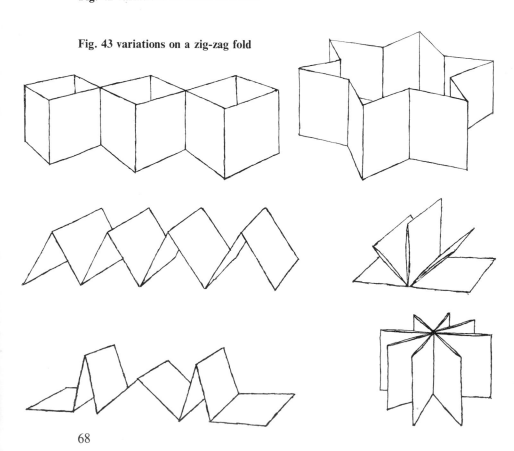

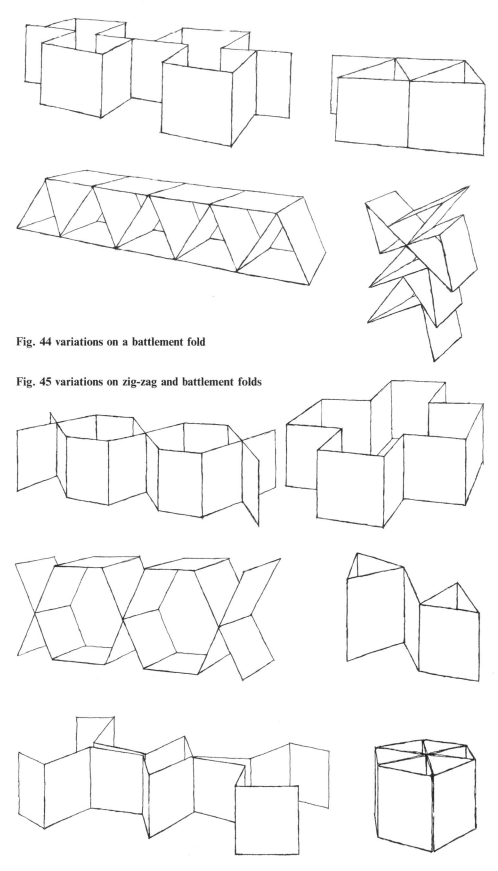

Fig. 44 variations on a battlement fold

Fig. 45 variations on zig-zag and battlement folds

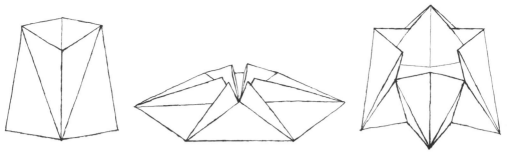

Fig. 46 variations on an arrowhead fold

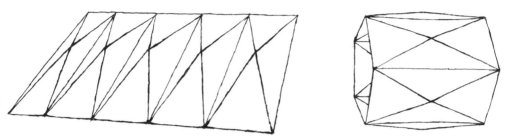

Fig. 47 variations on a diamond fold

Fig. 48 variations on rolled & curved shapes

By cutting and folding paper, you can discover a great variety of rigid shapes that can be grouped in different ways to make a raised design. The effect develops from the contrast of straight edges with slanted and flat planes. Figures 42–47 show a variety of shapes that can be built up from cutting and folding (see pp. 15–22 for the simple folds).

You can make a further range of shapes by rolling and curving paper and so developing an effect of curved edges and rounded planes (fig. 48).

There are countless variations and effects to explore using folded shapes alone, rolled and curved ones alone, or a combination of all of them. Make up the shapes as small or larger units and assemble them by bringing their edges or sides up to each other, by overlapping them, by building them up into more complex forms, or by fitting them together in some other manner. The pieces can be lying down or on edge, though if they project upwards too much they could bend and spoil. You may like to make a very low relief (about $\frac{1}{4}$ in.) and a higher one (about $1\frac{1}{2}$ in.). A great deal may be achieved with just one colour of paper (light and shadow will create their own strong interest among the forms) but any number of different coloured papers may be used if preferred.

When the combination of shapes has been decided upon, make them up separately, running a little glue down the edges of any shape that needs fixing, and gluing together any individual shapes that have to be joined to make a bigger one. Assemble all the final shapes loose on a table. Prepare a support (p. 30). Lightly glue the underneath of each of the shapes and transfer them to their place on the support, letting one dry before moving on to the next.

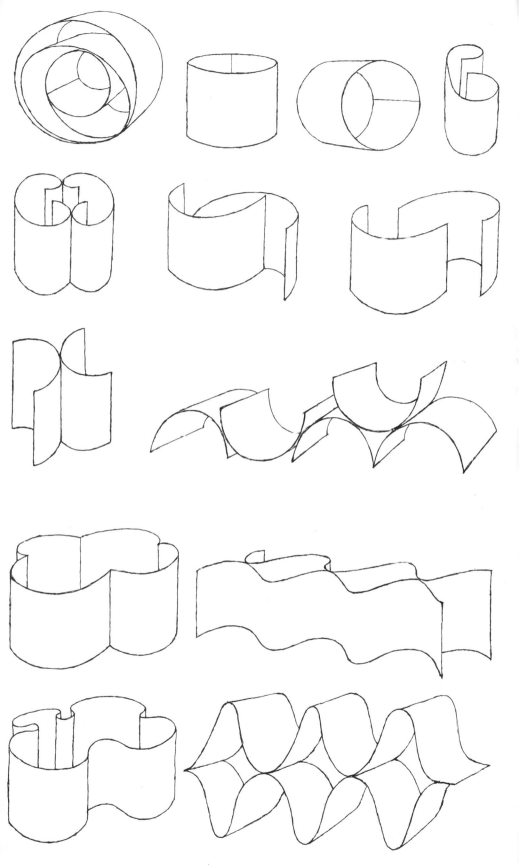

Fig. 49

As before, you can start with the support and build up a design to fit it. This is straightforward if the support is all one colour or texture, but if varied background areas are planned, the relationship of the shapes to the background must be thought out in advance.

The outbreak of fire in an apartment block (fig. 49) was made up of paper strips used lying down. The building shapes were cut from drawing paper, the flames from glazed brochure paper to give them added brightness. Strips of drawing paper were used standing on edge for the bride and groom (fig. 50). Both designs were mounted on cardboard covered with sugar (construction) paper.

Wave-formed

Paper: typing paper (thin cartridge or drawing paper; sugar or
    construction paper; pastel paper; good writing paper; a similar
    fairly stout, flexible paper)
Scissors (craft knife and cutting board)
Adhesive, spreader: a tube glue is suitable
Soft insulation or pinboard
Dressmakers' pins
Support and materials
    In the same way that a rock pool ripples and an ocean rises and falls

Fig. 50

with swelling waves, so paper can be curved to create a continuous flowing surface.

It is best to experiment first with strips of reasonably stout paper to see what kind of wave-formations result. Have a piece of soft insulation or pinboard handy, and some dressmakers' pins: cut a few straight and curved strips of paper and shape them into waves, pinning each wave temporarily as it is formed. The waves can be high or low, long or short. They can travel straight across the board, or curve away into a new direction: notice the different wave formations produced by making sharp or gradual turns. The end of a strip can lie flat or curve back under itself like a breaking wave. After experimenting with different shaped strips, cut out the main ones needed for the relief. Work out the arrangement by pinning them down lightly to the insulation board (the pin marks should be scarcely noticeable later). Now prepare a support of the right shape. As parts of the support may be seen through the arches of paper it is wise to give some thought to its colour and texture. Be sure it is dry and flat before proceeding. Transfer the pieces of paper to it. Fix just one part of each strip down at a time by gluing the support where the paper meets it and lowering the paper onto it. Use as little glue as possible: a thin line is enough. Too much glue will cause the paper between the waves to stick down and flatten. As the design develops it will suggest more and more clearly the shape of strips needed to complete it. Keep the paper clean throughout and avoid pressing down on any waves that have already been fixed into place.

Fig. 51 Relief by Louise, age 20   **Fig. 52**

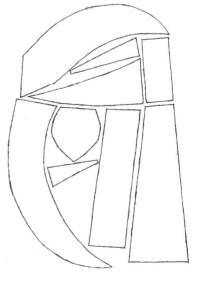

The strips of drawing paper making up the wave-formed relief (fig. 51) have been mounted and fixed against a background textured with plaster and sand to provide a contrast of surfaces. Fig. 52 shows the shapes of paper from which it was made up.

Curled

Any fairly firm paper
Scissors (craft knife and cutting board)
Adhesive, spreader: tube glue is suitable
Straight edge
A piece of insulation or pinboard (thickish cardboard)
Dressmakers' pins
Support and materials. Another piece of insulation or pinboard is
    suitable

The combining of loose and tight paper curls creates a surface of eddies and swirls very close to the movements of a river current and, with other flowing shapes, can be extended to produce all kinds of similar effects from the physical world that embody a sense of movement, be it spinning, whirling, cascading, gushing, winding or unwinding.

Cut a few strips of paper. They may be different lengths and widths, but it should be remembered that they will be fixed on edge and that their width will be the distance they will stand out from the background. If they project more than an inch or so, they could easily bend and be spoiled. Curl some of them so that they are fairly slack, and others so that they are tighter (p. 21). Lay them on edge together on a piece of insulation or pinboard in different arrangements—touching, flowing in and out of each other, or raised one on top of the other. Notice the kind of movement they suggest and how it might be developed. Use pins to keep them open temporarily or to hold in place any strips that lead off in other directions. (Tension will tend to close up the strip.) Make and add any further curls to complete the idea that develops.

Prepare a support. Glue the underside of one curl and transfer it to the support, keeping it lightly pressed down both in the position and at the tension that is required. Use pins to keep it from closing until it is properly glued. Transfer the remaining pieces one at a time to complete the design.

An alternative method would be to prepare the support first and work directly onto it, building up a design of curls and adding to it as necessary.

It will be possible, with a little practice, to anticipate results. Then is the time to develop designs from shaped strips, e.g. tapered, or with a decorative top edge (the bottom edge should remain straight for sticking to the support). These should open up new ideas.

angled 'curls'
Strips may be bent through angled turns to create a different sense of flow.

Fig. 53

Cut strips of a fairly stout paper and bend them sharply at increasing intervals, turning the strip always in the same direction. When it is unfolded and stood on edge it will form an expanding shape. A different kind of shape results from bending the strip at equal intervals and unfolding it. A number of such shapes placed side by side will produce a maze effect which can be varied by the height and colour of the papers and the way they meet, interlock or mount one above the other. Remember to keep them to a safe height.

Work out the arrangement on a table. The pieces will stand by themselves and keep position without pinning. Prepare the support (p. 30) and transfer them into place one at a time, gluing the under edges or sides and holding each one in place until it is stuck.

The fountain design (fig. 53) used both flowing and angled curls of drawing paper stuck to cardboard. The curls that project were secured with a bead of glue at key points.

Spiralled

Any fairly firm paper
Scissors (craft knife and cutting board)
Adhesive, spreader: tube glue is suitable
A piece of insulation or pinboard (thickish cardboard)
Dressmakers' pins
Matchsticks (similar thin sticks)
Support and materials

A circle or rounded shape of paper can be cut spirally into the centre to suggest a whirlpool. The spiral can be cut freehand or using lightly marked guide lines (dotted lines fig. 54a). Placed flat on the table the spiral is barely definable, but it can be raised into a relief form.

i Hold down the centre of the circle with one finger and slide the inner

Fig. 54

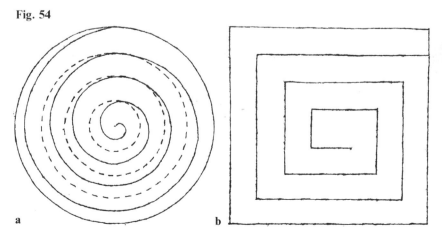

a   b

Fig. 55

spiral round to ride over it. A saucer-like form will begin to appear. Continue doing this in the same direction with the next spiral and a whirlpool will start to form in depth. If the outer spirals slide over the inner ones each time, a regular dished effect will be produced; if some slide over and others slide under the inner ones the effect will be irregular. To fix them in shape, glue the spirals at suitable points where they overlap, making sure each point is secure before sliding the next spiral round.

An arrangement of these shapes creates a surface of concave or convex forms, depending which way up they are positioned. They can be all one colour or several colours: light and shadow will play an important part in the finished effect either way.

When the shapes have been assembled, prepare a support (p. 30) and transfer them to it, gluing them at convenient points where they meet the flat surface or each other.

Different coloured pages from an old photograph album were used to make the design based on loudspeaker equipment (fig. 56). A further use of spiral 'saucers' can be seen in the form of the crab (fig. 68 p. 100).
ii Have a piece of insulation or pinboard or thickish cardboard handy and some dressmakers' pins. Cut out several spirals of the same or different colours. Lay a spiral on the pinboard. Hold down the outer end of the spiral with a finger-tip and keep it there. Pick up the centre and turn it over with the other hand to lie flat. Slide this centre end around, making the spiral take up different serpentine shapes. When you find a pleasing shape pin down both ends of the spiral to keep the shape in place. Do the same with another spiral and pin it down next to the first one so that they relate in an interesting way. Continue doing this with further spirals until the design is complete. Prepare a support (p. 30) and transfer the pieces to it one at a time, using a bead of glue to stick down the ends. This process has been used to suggest the feeling of the frightened bird in a cage (fig. 55).
iii Have the same materials ready as for the preceding section, together with a few matchsticks. Hold down the outer end of a spiral and pick up the centre: it will lift into a corkscrew shape. Support it temporarily from beneath the centre with a sharpened matchstick squared off to the required height and pushed into the pinboard. Do the same with another spiral and fix it to relate to the first one. Continue with further spirals until the design is complete. Prepare a support (p. 30). Cut a second set of sticks to the right height for each spiral, squaring off both ends this time. Transfer the first spiral to its place on the support. Glue down the outer tip. Glue both ends of the stick, raise the spiral and insert the stick vertically under the centre of the spiral. Hold it in place until it has stuck to both paper and support. Continue doing this with the rest of the spirals.

angled 'spiral'

Cut squares of a fairly stout paper the same or different colours and cut into them with straight cuts more or less parallel to the edges, turning at an angle each time until the centre is reached (fig. 54b).

You can develop this spiral in any of the three ways described on page 79. The angled spiral relief (fig. 57) was made with pastel papers and matchsticks fixed to cardboard.

Interlocked

Fairly firm paper
Scissors (craft knife and cutting board)
Adhesive, spreader: tube glue is suitable
Support and materials
(Straight edge; pencil)
Paper strips folded and curved in different directions can be arranged to form intricate interlocking designs.

a laid on edge
i Use fairly firm paper of one or more colours. Cut it into strips ranging

Fig. 56   **Fig. 57**

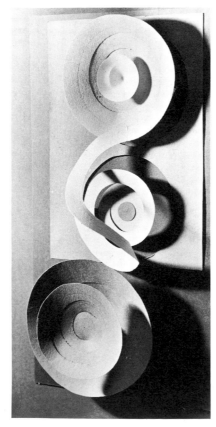 

Fig. 58

from about $\frac{1}{4}$–$1\frac{1}{2}$ in. wide. They can be the same or different widths, and each strip can vary in width along its own length as long as one edge is straight. Crease across the width of the strips, folding them backwards or forwards to take up a clockwise or anti-clockwise direction, or regular or irregular zig-zags as you wish. Stand them on edge, interlocking with each other. Experiment by trying them in various arrangements, re-creasing and folding them to fit in with any new directions that suggest themselves.

Prepare a support (p. 30) and transfer the pieces to it, gluing the under-edges and holding each one in place until it is stuck.

ii Cut strips as above and curve or coil them in different directions. Arrange them on edge, interlocking them to make a curving maze. Prepare a support (p. 30) and transfer the pieces to it. See note on curling, p. 75.

iii Make an interlocking design using both folded and curved strips.

F

Drawing paper and thin card were used to make the riverside warehouses and alleys (fig. 58). The river is creased carbon paper. Thin notebook paper was used to create the curling cloud effect above. The relief was built up on an off-cut of chipboard.

b laid flat
i Cut strips as for method **a**. This time there is no need to keep one edge straight. Crease and fold them into regular or irregular zig-zags. Lay them down flat on a table, some in one direction, others at right angles to them, crossing them under or over each other at suitable points to form a design of interlocking arches. Flatten some of the zig-zags if the design seems to need it. Prepare a support (p. 30) and transfer the strips to it, gluing lightly across the underneath parts of the strips where they touch the support. It is advisable to work out the best order for fixing down the strips so that the strips added later can easily be passed under and over those that are glued down first.
ii Cut strips as above. Crease and fold them as regular or irregular battlements (see p. 17). Arrange them into a design in which they cross each other, and transfer them to a support.
iii Cut strips as above. Curve them into continuous wave formations (see p. 21). Arrange them into a design in which they cross each other and transfer them to a support.
iv Make a design of interlocking arches using both folded and curved strips as above.

Ribboned

Ribboned paper: streamers (printers' trimmings; paper 'straw'; cut strips)
Scissors
Adhesive, spreader: paste is suitable
Support and materials
    Ribboned paper can create veiled or densely matted effects, fixed to remain in place or to hang free. Some papers are obtainable in ribboned or shredded form and others can be cut into long thin strips by folding or rolling a piece of paper several times and cutting across it in very narrow widths.
i Prepare a suitably shaped support (p. 30) and work with it propped upright. Select an assortment of coloured ribbons or streamers. Paste them by their ends to the support, starting at the bottom and working upwards, and letting them hang in their natural formations. Put a touch of paste behind any parts that need to be anchored more securely on the way up. They may be built up in a regular pattern or at random, and can be added one on top of the other to give greater depth and variety. Trim off any unwanted lengths. The ribbons can be secured so that they do not move, or they can be glued at the top only so that they will move in the breeze, creating a surface of changing colour and motion.
ii Work with the support flat, arranging and fixing the ribboned paper in any way that is convenient. The sea star (fig. 76) was made like this.

Landscaped

Fairly firm paper
Scissors (craft knife and cutting board)
Adhesive, spreader: tube glue is suitable
Straight edge
Compasses; pencil
Support and materials

Some of the ideas discussed under folded and curved paper can be developed with larger pieces to create a relief surface of continuous planes similar to landscape forms: the gently rising slope, the steep rock face, the ridging of mountains, the winding river bed. The inspiration lies not so much in the natural rendering of the features as in the geometry underlying them: the same live principle can be at work in both the landscape and the paper.

It is best to use fairly firm paper, probably of various colours. Cut a few fairly large shapes, making some symmetrical and others irregular. The following ideas may be worth exploring:

i Cut out a rectangle of paper. Score a returning arc inwards from one end, starting and finishing exactly at a corner. The arc should extend about a third of the way down the paper. Score a similar arc from the opposite end. Score a line straight down the centre of the paper through both arcs. Cut down this line from opposite ends of the paper as far as each of the arcs. Bend the paper sharply down from the scored lines, sliding the two pairs of cut edges over each other to raise a scalloped ridge form (fig. 59a). Glue the over-lapping edges.

ii Cut out a circle of paper. Mark four points at roughly equal intervals round the circumference. Cut in from each of these points about half way towards the centre. Overlap each pair of cut edges a little, and glue them, forming a rounded hill shape (fig. 59b).

iii Cut a wide strip of paper. Fold across it at varying intervals and at different angles, making an irregular zig-zag fold (p. 16). Flatten out the strip. Fold each of the long sides inwards about a quarter of the width of the strip. Cut along the zig-zag folds from the edges of the paper as far as the lengthwise folds. Overlap and glue the cut edges at opposite ends of each rising fold, making a chain of ridges. Cut straight along the glued overlap on both sides between the lowest points of the valleys to make the chain of ridges lie flat (fig. 59c).

iv Cut out a rectangle of paper. Score across between two diagonally opposite corners in a long 'S'. Raise the two sides from the scored line, working along it a little at a time and sharpening the crease as you do so. Bend one of the other corners under to meet the scored line, and press out a crease to meet the end of the 'S'. Fold the opposite corner under to meet the scored line from the other side, and press out to a crease to meet the other end of the 'S'. Turn the paper over and open the two side

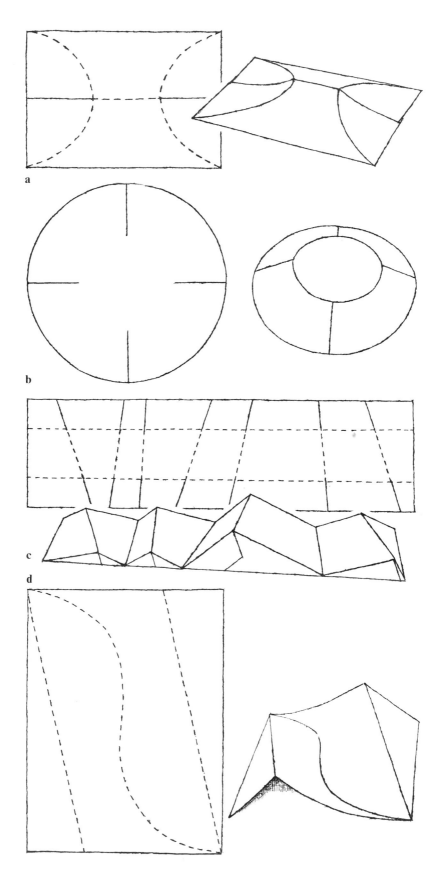

a

b

c

d

Fig. 59

folds to a wider angle. This will produce the start of a winding valley (fig. 59d). It may be necessary to fix it down with a touch of glue on the underneath edges.

You can discover innumerable landscape forms by scoring, folding and cutting paper in ways similar to the above. They can either be designed carefully to fit together, or they can grow together by trimming and shaping as each new part is added. Prepare a support (p. 30) and glue the pieces to it by their edges or by prepared flaps.

These processes can be developed to greater depth and scale to make a tableau model.

Pulped

Newspapers, kitchen paper and other soft papers can be soaked and mixed to a pulp with paste for modelling quite freely onto a support. The mixture is plastic while it is wet and can be shaped with considerable detail. It sets hard, retaining its shape as it dries, with only a slight shrinkage. It can be given greater density by adding ready-mixed plaster.

making the mixture
Newspaper (kitchen or shelf paper; a similar soft paper)
2 containers: buckets (bowls)
Cellulose or cold water paste
Plaster: builders' quality is suitable
Mixing and washing-up bowls
(Plastic sheet; steel wool; sand, sawdust or similar material)

Tear some newspaper or a similar paper into small pieces. Soak them in a container of water for a few hours, or boil them in a pan of water to soften them more quickly. Shred and pulp the paper thoroughly by working it with the hands. Squeeze out excess water and put the pulp in another container. Mix some paste in the first container (p. 23) and add it to the pulp, working it together well. It should not be too stiff or too sloppy. This can be used as it is, or with the addition of ready-mixed plaster.

To mix plaster you should pour a little water into a bowl and sprinkle the plaster onto it, distributing it evenly. *Do not stir it yet.* Continue adding plaster until it has risen level with the surface of the water. Now stir by hand, agitating the plaster from below the surface to avoid creating air bubbles. Dissolve any lumps that may have formed, though there should not be many if the plaster has been added evenly. The mixture is now ready to use, and should be used at once as it will begin to harden immediately. If a further mixing is needed, clean the mixing bowl thoroughly in a separate washing-up bowl, dry the hands, and add and mix the extra plaster. Wash the mixing bowl finally in the larger bowl. When the pieces have settled drain off the water and throw away the sediment. Do not pour the sediment down the sink. Steel wool in the sink outlet will prevent any plaster that *does* get in there from clogging it. A fitted sediment trap will prevent problems.

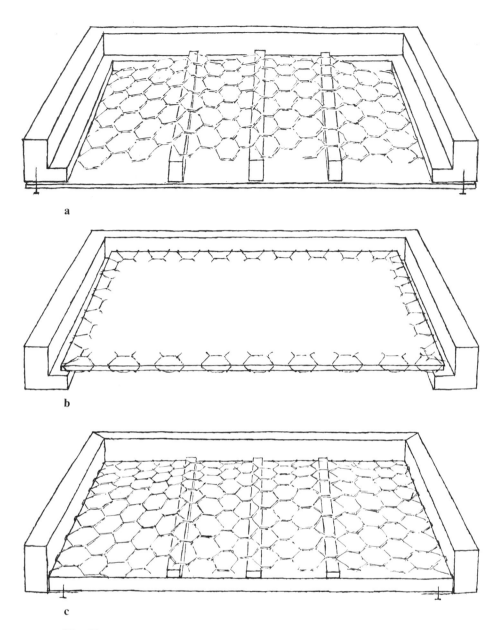

a

b

c

Fig. 60

The plaster would normally set fairly quickly—dental plaster or plaster of Paris very quickly, builders' plaster more slowly. Setting will be considerably delayed if the plaster is added immediately to the mixture of paste and paper, thus allowing ample time for working with it. A little sand, sawdust or similar ingredients may be added to give the mixture texture.

supports for the mixture
i   Chipboard (marine ply; pegboard; wood)
    Saw
    Sandpaper

Cut a stout board to shape, sandpapering the edges as necessary, and spread the mixture on it. Press it down firmly and level it ready for modelling. If it is not spread too thickly it should adhere to the support as it dries, though there is a chance that parts of it could lift away.

ii Frame
    Hardboard (pegboard; Masonite; a similar board)
    Saw
    Sandpaper
    Chicken wire
    Wire cutters (pliers; tin snips)
    Nails (panel pins)
    Hammer
    Pieces of wood

If a grip is provided for the mixture (fig. 60a) there will be no danger of it lifting away. Use an old picture frame with a simple right-angled moulding if possible. Cut a piece of hardboard or similar board the same size as the outside measurements of the frame, and sandpaper the edges. Cut a piece of chicken wire a little smaller than the board. Lay the frame face up and the chicken wire on it. Lay the board over them both and nail through it into the frame, securing the chicken wire between them. Turn the frame over and pull at the chicken wire a little to raise it in places from the board, tucking short lengths of wood under the mesh to keep it raised. This will help 'key' the mixture when it is added. Spread and press the mixture well down into the mesh and up into the edge of the frame. Level the surface ready for modelling.

iii Materials as above

Another way of using an old frame is illustrated in fig. 60b. Lay the frame face down. Cut a piece of hardboard or similar board to fit in it as a picture would. Cover the board with a slightly larger piece of chicken wire, so that it can be bent back all round behind the board. Lower this into the frame, mesh downward, and secure it with panel pins. Turn the frame face up and tuck short lengths of wood under the mesh to keep it raised. Spread and press down the mixture as above.

iv Chipboard (blockboard; wood)
    Saw
    Sandpaper
    Chicken wire
    Wire cutters (pliers; tin snips)
    Staples
    Hammer
    Battens (wood strips)
    Set square, pencil
    Screws, awl, screwdriver, countersink drill
      or oval nails (panel pins)
    Cellulose filler (U.K. Brummer stopping)
    Pieces of wood

Cut a piece of chipboard, blockboard or wood to the shape required and sandpaper the edges. Cover it with chicken wire as above, and secure the wire at the back with a few staples or panel pins. Cut battens or wood strips to fit round the sides of the support: they should be a little deeper than you intend the mixture to be. Mitre or butt-join them at the corners and fix them to the edges of the support with countersunk screws, oval nails or panel pins. Fill in any holes with cellulose filler or Brummer stopping, and sandpaper them flush when dry. Tuck short lengths of wood under the mesh to keep it raised (fig. 60c). Spread and press the mixture as above.

modelling the mixture
Thin paper, e.g. detail or kitchen paper
Drawing medium
Bodkin (sharpened match; cocktail stick; a similar tool)
Simple tools, e.g. knife, fork, spoon, chip of wood, large nail
Paint (ink; dye; spray; aerosol)
Wax polish (polyurethane varnish)
i The surface should be fairly level, though there is no need to smooth it down too much. Have some spare mixture handy in a bowl in case it should be needed. The surface may be modelled with the hands or with simple tools, and can be reduced or built up rather like clay. To sharpen

Fig. 61a

the edges of any shapes, draw the tip of a knife blade along them, pressing down with it to make a deeper impression. Many simple tools such as kitchen forks and spoons can produce a variety of impressions in the surface, or they can drag and work the surface into broken texture (this can be flattened slightly if it pulls away too much: it still has an interesting effect).

ii You may prefer to work out a careful design first. Make a drawing on *thin* paper, and prepare a support to size. Lay the mixture, smoothing off the surface as much as possible. Lower the design on it, face up, and press down gently to keep it in place. Using a bodkin or similar sharp point, prick through the outlines of the drawing at close intervals. Remove the paper and join up the prick marks with the tip of a knife. Model the surface as above, keeping the drawing to hand in case the lines should be smoothed or covered over with the modelling.

The colour of the mixture as it dries out may be quite pleasing and suitable for the relief as you planned it. If, however, it seems to need a further colour, wash or spray the surface with a water or emulsion paint, ink or dye. The correct colour can heighten the relief effect. Alternatively, the relief forms may be picked out in different colours. The dry surface can be given an attractive finish by working over it with a household wax or polyurethane varnish (see p. 26).

The rhinoceros and hedgehog reliefs (fig. 61) were modelled in a mixture

Fig. 61 b

of pulped paper and plaster, and tooled with simple kitchen implements. They were painted with powder colour and coloured inks.

Pasted in layers

Soft papers can be torn and pasted over a raised surface to form a 'skin' which can be removed when dry. You can make the raised surface in two different ways:

a   a modelled relief
Newspaper
A similar soft paper
Scissors
Paste
Flat bowl
Two boards
Hessian (burlap)
Clay (plasticine; permanently plastic modelling material)
Modelling tools
Paint (ink; dye; spray; aerosol)
Wax polish (polyurethane varnish)
Support and materials
   Spread clay about 1 in. deep on a board covered with hessian or burlap to prevent the clay sticking. Trim the clay to shape and model the surface with the hands or with simple tools, reducing and building it up to make the design. Avoid deep undercutting.
   Tear newspaper *and* a similar soft paper into strips or small pieces. Keep them in two separate piles. Fan out some of the newspaper pieces into a flat-bottomed bowl of water and when they are thoroughly wet, lay and press them gently down over all the modelled surface, covering it completely. Work the paper well into all the shapes, taking care not to flatten them. Water is the only binding agent used for this first layer, so as to prevent the paper from adhering too strongly to the clay. Now mix some paste in the flat-bottomed bowl. Fan out some pieces of the other paper into the paste and soak them well. Lay and press these down to cover the first layer, overlapping them all a little and ensuring that each piece is pressed down into the modelling as before. Work out any air or paste bubbles that become trapped. Through using this different kind of paper it will be easier to see when the whole area has been covered. Fan and soak some pieces of newspaper in the paste and cover the area with a third layer of paper. Using the two papers alternately, continue covering the surface until about six layers of paper have been built up—more if it is a very large area. For the final layer, use whichever kind of soft paper gives the effect you want. If the surface is to be painted the relief may simply be completed with the original papers.
   When the paper has dried out, lay another board on top of it and turn over the two boards together with the relief between them. Remove the modelling board, peel off the hessian, and remove the clay with a spoon,

a wire-ended modelling tool or any other suitable tool.

Turn over the layered paper skin: it will now be quite firm and can be trimmed and painted if required. It may be hung or glued as it is on a vertical surface. Alternatively, its effect may be enhanced by gluing it to a panel support.

b a constructed relief

Materials as above, but with scrap materials replacing the clay and modelling equipment. Suitable scrap would be: expanded polystyrene in the form of blocks or ceiling tiles; paper, cardboard or plastic cartons; wire; fabric; wire wool; foam plastic. You will also need tools to shape and fix these materials temporarily.

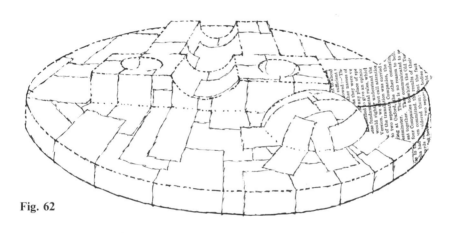

Fig. 62

Build up on a board an arrangement of shapes to be covered by the paper skin. Keep the shapes fairly low and the arrangement simple to start with. Forms may be filled out with a soft packing material as necessary. Secure the various pieces in place temporarily with adhesive, adhesive tape, pins or clips. Work over the whole surface with alternate layers of paper as above (fig. 62). When the paper is dry, turn the relief over and remove the supporting pieces of scrap. If some have stuck fast to the paper, simply remove as much as possible: the remaining parts will probably not affect the result. In fact, if they are light enough, they need not be removed at all. Complete the relief as above.

Metal foil

A characteristic of metal foil sheeting, like oven foil, is that it can be moulded to fit close round other forms and can be pressed into cavities and apertures so that it takes their shape. You can use this characteristic to good advantage in making a relief or engraving.

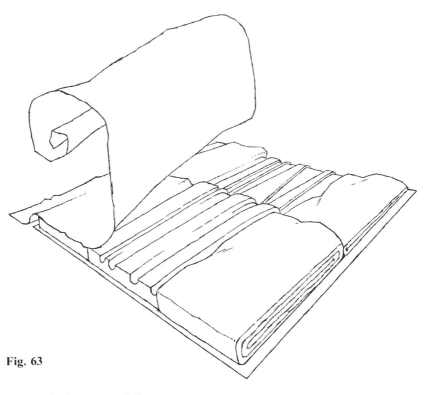

Fig. 63

a a raised paper relief

Any thick paper
Scissors
Paste, brush
Drawing medium
Knife
Sheet of metal foil ·
Blunt tool: bone folder (lollipop stick; a similar tool)
Support and materials
(Figured or textured paper)

i Draw a design on a sheet of paper to act as a guide while the relief is being made. Keep the design simple.

Prepare a support from hardboard, Masonite or a similar firm board (p. 30). Tear or cut out from any thick paper the main shapes of the design, and paste them down, referring to the drawing as necessary. Be ready to modify this from time to time if the paper shapes suggest it. Build up the shapes by pasting on further layers or wads of paper trimmed to size, raising the different areas to the level you want: some will be in low relief, others higher. Work the tip of a knife along any edges that need to be more sharply defined. You can introduce final textural effects by using a strongly textured paper as the top layer, e.g. figured doilies, embossed wallpaper.

When the paper has dried out, lay a sheet of metal foil over it. It should be about 1 in. larger all round. Press it into the modelled forms with the fingers, working it well down into all the detail. A blunt tool such as a bone folder will be a useful aid with some of the fine detail. Too much pressure will make the foil split. The foil should retain all the features of your modelling. Turn the edges of the foil back behind the support and smooth them into place.

ii A more direct method of forming the paper is to make it into wads, rolls and other shapes for building up a relief surface on which to mould the foil sheet. Use almost any kind of paper for this. To make a wad, fold a sheet of paper into several thicknesses; brush paste generously in between the main layers and press the wad out flat. If paste squeezes out round the edges, so much the better: it will help stick it all together. Keep it as flat as possible while it is drying. The wad can then be trimmed to any shape. To make a roll, paste sheets of paper together and roll them up tightly. Leave it to dry into the form you want, i.e. round, flattened, bent. This can be trimmed to shape later.

Arrange and build up these shapes into a relief and paste them to a support. When it is dry, you can mould the foil over it (fig. 63).

b   an engraving
Newspaper
Scissors
Paste, spreader
Sheet of metal foil
Blunt point: knitting needle (old ball-point pen; pencil crayon;
    matchstick; shaped piece of wood)
(Paint)

The light-reflecting surface of metal foil gives a special quality to lines engraved on it. The foil has to be stretched flat over a pad of softened material and the lines impressed into it through the foil. When the pad hardens, the impressions become fixed.

The pad can be made from newspaper. Paste several layers together to a shape a little smaller than the sheet of metal foil. Lay the foil over the newspaper, smooth it out flat, and turn it under round the edges. Make a design on it by pressing with a slightly blunted point, being careful not to puncture the foil. The impressed design will remain when the pad dries.

The engraving may be coloured with a wash of transparent oil paint thinned with turpentine, a drying oil, or polyurethane varnish. The wash should be thin enough for the sheen of the metal foil to shine through and give the colour lustre.

With plaster

Sheet of firm paper or metal foil
Scissors (craft knife and cutting board)
Adhesive, spreader: glue is suitable
Board
Plaster, see below
Mixing bowl, washing-up bowl
Sandpaper
Coloured ink (dye; water colour; powder or poster paint; emulsion
    paint); brush
Tools for making paper shapes; clay (plasticine)
Support and materials

Fig. 64

Paper and metal foil can both be used as moulds for taking plaster casts. The paper should be reasonably firm.

i Crumple a sheet of paper or foil with different pressures. Open it out a little and lay it flat on a board (fig. 64). If you have made a paper mould, use quick-setting plaster of Paris or dental plaster; if it is a foil mould, it is possible to use ordinary builders' plaster instead (see p. 85). Mix the plaster and pour it carefully into the mould to fill up all the depressions, levelling off the surface as far as possible. Watch that the plaster does not spill too much over the edges of the sheet. When the plaster has set hard, sandpaper the top surface. Break out the whole cast, or take individual shapes from it. Make any further moulds and casts as necessary, and arrange the pieces together to form a relief design. Cut a support to size and transfer the pieces to it, gluing them in place. Colour-wash the plaster if you wish with coloured ink, dye, or a water colour.

ii You can make and use as moulds a variety of individual shapes built from strong paper (see p. 84). They can be cast as described above and then assembled and mounted to form a relief. The under-edges of some of the paper moulds may need supporting with wedges of clay or plasticine or by some other means for the short time the plaster takes to set.

6   Using paper for modelling

Some of the many ways in which paper can be made into flat and relief shapes have already been investigated. These and other processes can be used to create works in space. These may be:

standing on their own: the shape must be made rigid by the method of folding, curving or forming

standing with the help of a support (see p. 31)

suspended (see p. 31)

rotating: by securing it to a turning support or arranging for it to turn on a fixed one (see p. 32)

moving freely: by providing the means of movement

Be sure to choose the right kind of paper for the job. All kinds of paper can be used, though some are clearly better for certain work than others: an unsuitable paper could lead to disappointment. Decide whether the work is to stand, hang, rotate or move in some other way, and keep this in mind throughout, providing for its support at the most convenient stage.

Crumpled and tied

a   without support
i   Soft paper
  Scissors
  Paste, brush, bowl
  Thread (twine)
  Covering materials: thin paper (butter muslin; cheesecloth; a similar light fabric; fibres; dried plants; shavings: various kinds of scrap) adhesives as required; paint (ink); texturing materials

By bunching soft papers and binding them with thread it is possible to make a simple shape complete in itself or forming part of a larger one.

If you are making one complete shape, make sure the sheet of paper will be large enough: it is surprising how small even big pieces become when you begin to tie them. Crumple the paper and bunch it into a shape that is as near as possible to the shape you want. Tie thread or twine loosely round it. Make up any further pieces that you need to add and work them into the shape. Bind all the parts more securely, tightening the thread to pull them in where needed: the tightness of the thread emphasizes the shapes that result. Fig. 65 shows the form of a fisherman at this early stage and also suggests how it might be set up finally to include a net of woven paper and a boat house of corrugated paper.

You can finish the tied model by covering it with pasted paper. Soak strips of newspaper in paste and lay them over and round the form, covering it completely with a paper 'skin'. Work the strips into place with both hands, holding the model bodily if possible. Do not press too hard in case the underlying shape is distorted, but make sure the strips are well stuck down. Continue laying and binding strips to fill out the surface form and strengthen the skin. It may be necessary to cover the

Fig. 65

model quite a few times, especially if it is on the large side. Even at this stage, more paper may be crumpled and added if further modelling is needed.

When the form is finished, leave it to dry: it may take a day or so unless it can be placed in a drying cabinet or some other warm place. Paint or texture it (pp. 26–28).

Alternatively, the basic paper shape may be covered with butter muslin, cheesecloth, net, or a similar light fabric; or you could build other materials onto it, such as teased rope or fibre, dried leaves, grasses and other plant forms, or scrap of various kinds. Some of these may want a slightly stronger adhesive.

You can also assemble separately crumpled and tied shapes into a more complex form. Work out how each shape can contribute to the whole, and allow any extra length for tucking in or for fixing in some other way while making it up. Assemble the parts in the most convenient order. They may be bound together, wrapped, fitted into each other, or joined together in any manner the form suggests, with a support if needed. The assembled form may be covered or treated as described above.

Paper made up into round or flattened rolls may also be tied and assembled in a variety of ways to build up complex shapes. They can be covered and treated in the same ways as above.

ii Materials, as above, i
  Old stockings (tights; plastic bag; a similar article)
  Needle (adhesive, spreader; stapler)
You can make forms by packing and tying soft paper into a variety of articles such as used stockings, tights and plastic bags. The forms are likely to be very simple, but, by packing and tying carefully, one can vary them considerably. Knowing the kind of shapes that result, it is possible to plan a work that uses their particular quality.

Crumple the paper and use it to fill out the different parts of the form. Close up the end by sewing, gluing or stapling. Tie the form tightly or loosely with thread or twine to keep the parts in position and to pull them in where necessary. The tightness of tying determines the final character of the form. The new-born baby (fig. 66) is an example of a form at this stage; the cot was made of rolled paper (p. 21).

Cover and complete the model as described above.

As before, it is possible to make up a number of packed shapes and assemble them into a more complex form by tying, sewing or gluing them.

b with support
i Materials, see p. 95
  Wire and cutters for the support.
Crumpled or rolled paper can be built into a wire support. This allows greater control of the modelling and makes it more rigid.

Use a fairly flexible galvanized wire (about gauge 18) a few feet long. Bend and form it into a shape, making each of the main parts into a loop, and twisting any further lengths of wire onto the standing end as

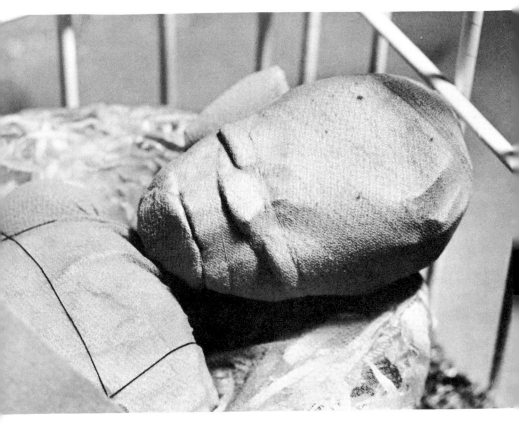

Fig. 66

work progresses (fig. 67a). The shape can be flat or it can be built outwards to extend the loops in other directions. If the finished model is to stand, the wire framework should also be able to stand at this stage. Alternatively, you should have a clear idea as to how it is to be set up.

Crumple newspaper or a similar paper into compact 'parcels' and work them into the wire loops. Each parcel should fit fairly firmly and stay in place. Make it roughly the size and shape required for the finished model. As the packing and shaping of each part is finished, bind it into place with strong thread, twine or fine wire (florists' wire is useful for this): bind round both the paper and supporting wire, securing the binding with an extra twist round the support whenever necessary to prevent it slipping and to make the ends fast. Complete all the parcels in this way (fig. 67b). Fill in any gaps between the parcels or build further ones on if necessary. The overall shape of the parcelled framework should look something like the shape that you are aiming at finally. Cover and complete the model in the way described on page 97. Fig. 67c shows the wire and paper form finished. It was given a final

Fig. 67

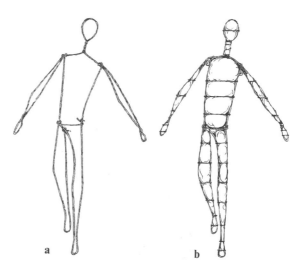

a   b

c

99

Fig. 68

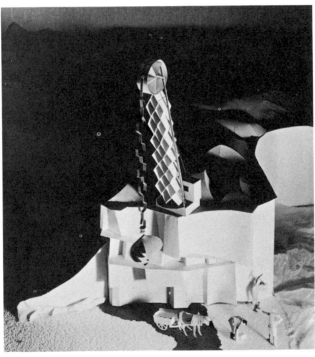

Fig. 69 Quarry,
by Elizabeth,
age 17, and the
author

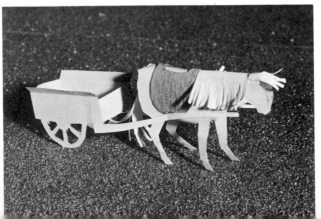

Fig. 70

layer of black tissue, which was also crumpled to make the hair. The dress and accessories were made of typing paper, the skipping rope of wire bound round with shreds from paper packing straw.

ii A support can be made using suitable rigid materials, e.g. wood; metal; chicken wire; scrap of various kinds. Crumple and tie the paper to it to fill out the forms, and complete the model as above.

Folded, rolled and curved

Paper formed into shapes by folding, rolling, curving and cutting (see pp. 68–71) can be assembled in an endless variety of ways to create experiences in space. The shapes can be expressively simple or organized into a more complex structure. The interest lies in the forms and surfaces themselves, their movement, and in the changes that take place under different lighting.

a without support
Firm paper
Materials and tools, see p. 67
   Use a fairly firm paper. The shape should support itself, except for a thread if it is to hang, or a simple pivoting arrangement if it is to rotate.

i Make a single shape by means of one or more of the processes illustrated on pp. 15–22. It can be made to spring from a certain point, to open out or close up like a flower, to turn or spin like a weather cock or float like a dart.

ii Make a number of shapes as above to fit together into a more involved form. Join the shapes by fitting one inside the other or by interlocking them. (The tension of curled papers, for example, may be enough to lock two together.) Alternatively, glue them with a bead or fine line of adhesive where the parts meet. Use adhesive only when absolutely necessary, and then very sparingly: apply it where it has most effect, which may sometimes be along an edge. The simplest shapes, even shapes of the same kind, can combine to form surprisingly complex designs by setting them against each other in different positions. The crab's limbs (fig. 68) were made from rolled drawing paper (p. 21), the shell from two spiral saucer forms (p. 77). The net was woven from strips of brown wrapping paper. The quarry scene (fig. 69) also illustrates a variety of processes. The sides of the quarry have been built up from irregularly cut battlement folds; the crane from zig-zag, battlement and roll-over folds; the workmen from folded paper; the donkey and cart from folded and curved paper (see detail, fig. 70). The view above the quarry shows uses of landscaped (see pp. 83–85) and crumpled paper.

iii Cut a sheet of paper as described on p. 39iii. Turn it to make a standing or hanging shape, either rounded or square-sided. The effect will depend largely on lighting from outside or from a light fixed up inside the shape.

b with support

Any paper

Materials and tools, see p. 67

Support and materials

You will generally need a fairly firm paper, but since the work is supported by other means, any paper can be used. Ideas for the structure and the kind of support needed can be worked out carefully first, and the paper shapes made and assembled to bring the idea to life. Alternatively, shapes can be built up freely on a prepared support, growing as each stage suggests the next. It is often a good idea to start with only a general idea of what you want; the way the paper takes shape and the forms come together can give fresh impetus and animation to the idea.

The materials chosen for the support should be in keeping with your plans for the paper. It may have to be light but rigid, flexible, single-stemmed, branched, in the form of scaffolding or an enclosed transparent shape, or in some other arrangement that will support the pieces. It may be either visible or concealed. Give it some thought: it is central to the whole work. Plan how the pieces are to be fixed to it: this may affect the way you make them, especially if the support is to enter or pass through them: the piece may have to be made around the support or with means of attachment included in it.

In general, keep any supporting structure as light, stable and well balanced as possible, relative to the scale of the work as a whole.

A work of this kind can have the ingenuity of machinery or elaborate architecture; it can be an abstract definition of space or movement or evolve a profusion of natural growth. Its character lies in the behaviour of the paper and the way this is used in organizing the shapes.

Unlimited inspiration for both unsupported and supported work lies in the rich variety of plant forms. Paper has something of the quality of living plants: it can be light, flexible, many-coloured and often transparent. Without any attempt being made to imitate the originals, paper can develop shapes very close to them, creating a 'flower-like' feeling which has an attraction of its own. The shapes of countless different flowers will suggest quite naturally a particular method of using paper; the trumpet of the greater bindweed and daffodil; the bell of the foxglove and campanula; the flopping petals of the poppy; the curling petals of the tiger-lily; the curved sheath of the wild arum; the tousled head of the chrysanthemum; the ordered symmetry of the dahlia. Leaf shapes will do the same: the spear of the teasel and iris; the twisting spikes of the thistle and holly; the crinkled primrose; the jagged edge of the dandelion; the smooth edge of the water-lily; and all the different 'cut' edges of leaves that spring singly or clustered about a stem. And there are other forms: cones and acorns and the winged sycamore; the fan of ferns; the plump stools of fungi; the many strange growths of cacti. These and almost the whole flower kingdom can be expressed in some way with paper.

Any glimpse into a garden or greenhouse, a wayside lane or hedgerow, or even into an illustrated book of flowers, will give ideas for experiment.

Fig. 71   Fig. 72   Fig. 73

The petals of the chrysanthemums and daisies (fig. 71) were made by cutting into circles of light paper and gently curling them alternate ways. The bell flower (fig. 72) was made by cutting and folding. The opened shape at the bottom of fig. 72 shows how this was done. The bindweed trumpet (fig. 73) was formed from a simple cone, scored to fold back round the lip. The leaves are simply lightly scored shapes.

In the same way, paper of all kinds can be used to make clothes for occasions such as fancy dress parties, plays and carnivals, and for dressing models, dolls and puppets. The paper would need to be strong and flexible enough for the kind of wear expected of it. The garment should be fairly loose-fitting and cut to allow any movement of the limbs. Fig. 74 shows possible uses of paper for dressing up a Boy Prince. A glance through the processes in the book will suggest many ideas for making other kinds of costume.

Many other forms can be made to stand, hang, rotate or move freely. These include turning vanes, balloons, kites, flying darts, parachutes and other suspended or air-borne bodies.

Fig. 74 paper costume
Crown: rolled and cut paper (p. 14)
Hair: curled paper (p. 21)
Collar: fan folded paper (p. 18)
Cloak: ribboned paper, built up in layers (p. 82)
Tunic top: paper doilies or paper cuts (p. 38)
Arm bands: rolled paper, decorated with small cones (pp. 21–22)
Skirt: zig-zag folded paper (p. 16)
Leggings: spiralled paper (p. 77)
Shoes: half cones (p. 22) on flat sandals, decorated with cut paper fringes

Fig. 75

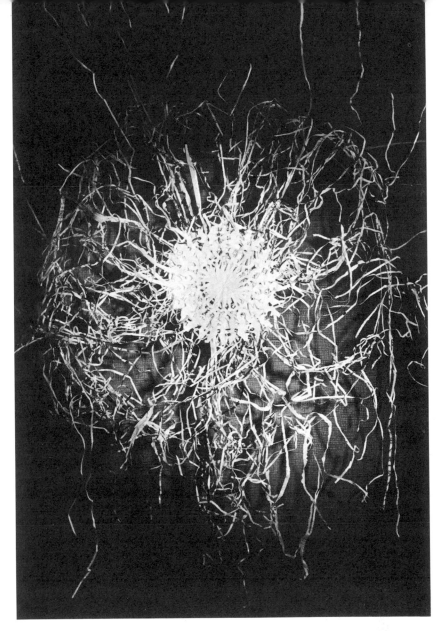

Fig. 76

Curled and spiralled

Materials, see pp. 75, 77
(Support and materials)

Curled and spiralled forms (pp. 75–80) can be made up either with or without support in the ways described in the section on reliefs. Curling or spiralling shapes may suggest an idea or the means of expressing an idea that you already have in mind. A few touches of adhesive may be sufficient to combine a number of shapes, or you may have to make a light framework to support them. Fig. 77 (p. 107) includes a simple example of curled paper in the form of a sea-anemone. A scored spiral may become a snake (fig. 75) and two spiral saucer forms may make up a crab's shell (fig. 68).

Fig. 77

Interlocked

Materials, see p. 80
(Support and materials)
Interlocking pieces (see p. 81) can be made up into a free-standing or hanging form. As before, the effects of interlocking will give ideas for starting or working out a form, and the pieces can be glued or supported according to how it develops.

Ribboned

Materials, see p. 82
(Support and materials)
Ribboned paper (see p. 82) can be made up into a free-standing or hanging form. Because of its nature, it will almost certainly need a support of some kind, although this may be no more than a thread on which it hangs or a light framework. You will need to glue the ribbons at certain points either to each other or to a supporting material. The sea-star (fig. 76) was built up on a wire hoop and the ribbons held together at the centre back and front by folded paper cuts (p. 38).

Landscaped

Materials, see p. 83
(Support and materials)
There are endless possibilities for developing a form from landscaped shapes (see p. 83). It may be made from a single shape or from a combination of shapes glued or fixed together (see fig. 59). It could well be self-supporting, as paper shaped like this can be quite rigid; but again, the nature of the work will suggest what is needed.

See-through forms

Materials, see p. 49
(Support and materials)
An arrangement of see-through shapes (see p. 49) can be put together to make a three-dimensional form. Each shape will have to be carefully considered and cut in relation to the rest, as each one will influence the lighting-effect of the others. They can be joined with adhesive or by using a suitably concealed framework. It may be possible to cut the shapes from the sides of a paper or cardboard container if the surface can be supported from underneath during the cutting.
Paper with pierced designs like cake doilies can be cut and made up into interesting effects. The fish and coral (fig. 77) were made with doilies on a light wire support. Fig. 78 shows the wire support used for the fish which was later decorated with black tissue paper and Honesty seed pods.

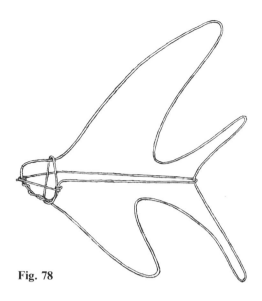

Fig. 78

Transparent forms

Materials, see p. 51
Support and materials
(shellac; dope; lamp)

Transparent papers can be stretched and fixed across an open-work support to make a construction of bright, clear colours.

Make a light framework using wire, balsa wood, cane, reed or cardboard. Stretch the papers across and round it, overlapping them for different effects and sticking them to each other or to the framework, whichever is appropriate. Kites and other forms turned by the wind can be made in this way, using thin cane or bamboo and painting the paper with shellac or aero-modelling dope. Soak canes or reeds in a sink to

Fig. 79

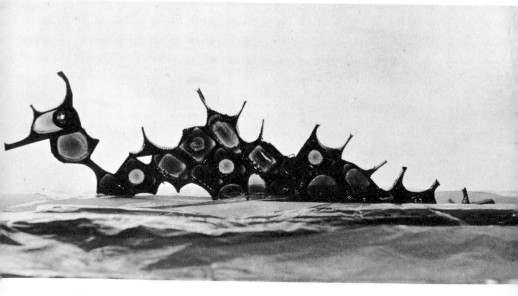

make them supple, and shape them while they are damp.

A cardboard box, a plastic bottle, or a similar container can make a support. Cut away parts of the sides and glue transparent papers across the openings so that light can show through them either from outside or from a lamp fitted inside.

Examples of the use of transparent papers can be seen in fig. 79. The sea-serpent was made from a cellophane candy separator cut along the different divisions to give the desired shape; the lake is coloured cellophane supported on wave-formed wallpaper. Further examples of the use of transparent forms are included in fig. 77. The jellyfish is clear cellophane; the starfish was cut from a light plastic bag and filled with dry seeded grass. The texturing on the arms was produced with split peas and pine needles.

Pulped

Pulped paper, used alone or mixed with plaster, makes a soft modelling material. It can be modelled broadly or in some detail to stand on its own or with a support.

a   without support
Materials, see p. 85
Modelling board: hardboard (tile; a similar firm surface)
(Adhesive, spreader; hand drill; craft knife)

Prepare the mixture, adding plaster if you wish (see p. 85). Work on a piece of hardboard or a similar surface on which the model can stay while it is drying. Squeeze some of the mixture into a lump and shape it with the hands, much as you would model clay, reducing it or adding to it from the rest of the mixture. Any pieces that you add should be firmly pressed into the main form to make sure that they key into it and will not loosen or come away later. The model should be firmly based with the greater weight at the bottom. Avoid making any part of it too thin: even if a thin part stays in place for a while, it could break off when it dries out. Any simple tool may be used for modelling the form further or for creating surface effects; knives, forks and spoons, lollipop sticks and other everyday articles are all useful.

The model could take a few days to dry naturally. It will do so much more quickly in a warm oven or in a heated drying cabinet (small pieces will take under half an hour). Stand it on oven foil or a similar material so as to prevent it sticking to the shelf.

If the surface is left as it is, the paper and plaster will dry out to produce interesting effects. If it is to be coloured, use a water-based or emulsion paint, ink or dye. A final coat of wax or polyurethane varnish could give it an attractive finish and seal it from possible damp. If an oil-based paint is to be used, size the model first, as it is quite absorbent and would simply soak up the paint.

It is possible to introduce other objects or materials into the shape at any stage during the wet modelling: press the mixture in firmly round

Fig. 80 Owl alighting, by Stephen, age 15

them to make them secure. If you want to add more pieces after the model is dry, drill or cut into it so as to insert them firmly. You can also glue other materials to the surface at this stage if necessary (see p. 33).

b with support

Materials as above
Support and materials, see below

Modelling onto a support naturally strengthens the finished work and provides opportunities of shaping the form in a greater variety of ways. The mixture adheres well to most kinds of support and does not shrink or crack round it as it dries.

This list of supports also gives suggestions for the kind of work that could be modelled on them:

A wood or metal rod fixed in a base: a simple upright model without too much projecting from it;

A wood or metal framework of upright and cross pieces: a more complex model, projecting wherever there is a cross piece for support;

A framework of strong cane, reed or rigid wire: any model that the arrangement and strength of the framework can support;

A core of stout rolled cardboard: a simple upright or horizontal model;

A firm construction of off-cut or scrap materials such as hardboard,

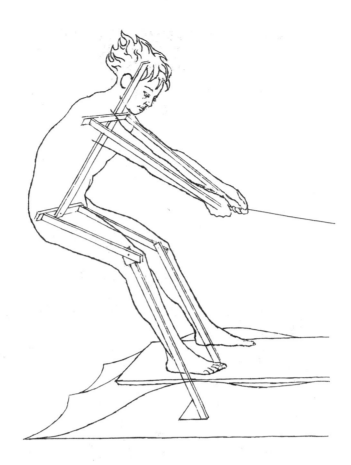

Fig. 81

pinboard, chipboard, wood, hard plastic, metal, chicken wire or other
metal mesh—fixed together by any suitable means: any model that the
arrangement and strength of the construction can support;

A single object such as a bottle, a can, a small branch, an irregular
stone or shell: a simple model dependent on the form underneath.

If you are constructing a support, be sure that it is secure: the paper
and plaster mixture is quite heavy while it is wet and will, of course,
damp the support, causing any absorbent material it contains to soften
temporarily. Prepare the mixture and model it on the support, pressing
it firmly into place all round. If you build on too much at a time and the
support is overloaded, the mixture could fall away or bend the support.
It would be better to wait for the first modelling to dry before building
on the rest. The finished form can be coloured or treated in any of the
ways discussed above (p. 109).

In fig. 80 pulped paper has been modelled onto a framework of scrap
to make an owl alighting. All the tooling was done with a kitchen knife
and fork. Fig. 81 shows a wooden framework designed to support a
water skier.

c moulded
Materials, see p. 85
Ready-made mould (materials for making a mould, see below)

111

The pulped paper and plaster mixture is soft enough to press into simple moulds for casting. Found objects such as plastic containers or half of a grapefruit skin may be used as moulds.

Alternatively, it is easy to make a mould of your own. Model or carve a shape from a firm vegetable or from a soft material such as clay or plasticine. Keep the shape very simple, with no undercutting. Place it on a board and build a low wall of clay or plasticine round it, leaving a gap of about 1 in. between the wall and the shape. Mix plaster of Paris or dental plaster into a thick cream (see p. 85) and pour it slowly over the modelled shape, letting it flood to the low wall. Build up the plaster until it is about 1 in. thick and flatten the top slightly. Let the plaster set thoroughly before turning the whole thing over. Remove the board and then the modelled shape. The plaster mould is now ready. Using a piece of cloth, grease the inside of the mould with Vaseline or petroleum jelly. It is now ready. Make up the paper and plaster mixture and pack it in. Let it dry out completely, then ease it from the mould with a knife blade. Small parts of the surface may come away on the mould, but if they do, the damage to the cast can be repaired with a little more of the mixture.

The cast may be interesting as it is, or can be assembled with others into a larger work. It can be coloured in the same way as a model (p. 26).

Pasted in layers

Strips or pieces of soft paper can be pasted in layers to a three-dimensional support which may afterwards be removed or left as part of the finished work.

a   with temporary support
i   Materials, see p. 90 (only one board needed)
   Craft knife (hard-backed razor blade)
Paper used in this way becomes hard when it dries and retains the shape in which it sets. If it is built up and allowed to harden on an underlying form that can be removed afterwards, it will stay up unsupported. Make a model using clay, plasticine or any permanently plastic modelling material. While this is still soft, cover it with alternate layers of newspaper and a similar paper (see relief, p. 90). When the paper covering is quite dry, cut round the centre line with a sharp blade, cutting right through into the modelling material. If the model is rather complicated, you may want to cut round some of the secondary forms as well. Turn the model on end and clear away as much of the clay as possible. Ease the main sections apart (fig. 82) and finish clearing out the clay. Do the same with any other sections that have had to be cut.

Re-assemble the sections and join them by pasting strips of paper in layers down the edges that meet, smoothing them down to blend with the rest of the surface. When it is all dry again, the model may be painted or textured (pp. 26–28).
ii   Materials, see p. 91
Make a construction from materials that can be removed from the paper

112

Fig. 82

skin when it is dry (see relief, p. 91). Cover the construction with alternate layers of paper and complete the work as above.

b   with permanent support
Materials, see p. 110
   You can construct a model using any light materials and covered with layers of pasted paper as above, leaving the construction as a support for the finished work.
i   As above, **a ii**. As the pieces will not have to be removed afterwards, they may be secured with greater freedom.
ii   A framework of rigid materials may be designed to play a visible part in the finished work. The framework should provide adequate surfaces or supports for the pasted strips.

Fig. 83

Cover the construction with alternate layers of paper (p. 90), and complete the model by painting or texturing if required.

Metal foil forms

A sheet of metal foil can be modelled into all kinds of shapes with the hands or with the help of simple tools. It is very pliable, but can be squeezed and worked to stay in position. Individual foil wrappers from confectionery, biscuits and other foods are also useful. There is a great variety of bright colours from which to choose. Some papers may need a touch of glue under parts that tend to lift.

114

i Metal foil
Scissors (craft knife and cutting board)
Adhesive, spreader
Tweezers

Make a complete form from a sheet or piece of foil. Cut into the foil from any direction that will make it easier to model the separate parts of the form. Tuck and press in any further pieces needed to develop it. A pair of tweezers will be useful for the smaller details in the modelling. The fox (fig. 83) was modelled from one sheet of foil and the foil moon provides a link in the background.

ii Materials as above
Tissue paper (cotton wool; kapok; a similar material); balsa wood (scrap of various kinds)—tools to shape them
Support and materials

Make a form from a sheet of foil, packing out some of the parts with a soft material such as twisted tissues or cotton wool, or moulding it round harder materials such as balsa wood or shapes of scrap.

iii Materials as above, **i, ii.**

Make up a number of shapes as above and combine them into a bigger one by nipping their meeting edges together, by gluing, or by some other suitable means.

Paper and foil casts

Materials, see p. 93
(Support and materials)

Paper and foil may be used to make moulds for three-dimensional work (see p. 94). Take casts from crumpled paper or foil or from mould shapes made up individually. Assemble them into a form by gluing them together or by running a thin coat of plaster between them and pressing tight. Pairs of shapes joined in this way can be built on to further pairs to create a more complex form. It could stand by itself, or be supported with added plaster or by a rigid material such as dowelling or stout wire.

7 Working in a group

A group achievement differs from that of an individual, not only in scale (it can be much more ambitious) but also in character, taking, as it does, something from all the contributions: there could be a variety of ideas and styles that have to adjust to each other, fitting together to make the finished work.

Members of a group can work side by side on a single job, developing it together through its various stages, or they can each make something of their own as part of a common project. All the work so far discussed may be organized as a group activity. In most cases, the method of organization would be clear from the nature of the work.

Organizing such a group depends on the kind of work, the materials, the numbers involved and the space available. Be sure there are enough papers, adhesives, tools and other materials, room for everyone to use them, and easy access to cleaning facilities. The group should be encouraged to discuss plans—what they aim to do, how they can do it, and what part each of them is responsible for. When everyone is clear about this, they can make a start.

Working together

A group activity involving everyone simultaneously on one project is a social occasion, calling for both initiative and compromise as the work proceeds. There will be continual discussion and a good deal of give and take. Ideas will be exchanged and approaches modified so that they all grow together as a whole. One or two individuals in the group may take a lead, but everyone is involved in carrying out his own share and in deciding how best he can adapt it to the general aim.

a a wall design

A group can build up a design together using most of the flat and relief processes described in the book, though some (such as collage, mosaic, and crumpled paper) are obviously more suitable than others. In some relief processes, the pieces will have to be made up separately.

If the group is to work direct onto the wall, the highest parts should be comfortably within reach. This should normally mean within reach from the floor for the convenience of picking up materials and tools and at a suitable height for reviewing progress by standing back from time to time. If the working surface extends higher, have a few sturdy kitchen tables or steps handy for standing on, and arrange for materials and tools to be accessible without too much clambering about or disturbance. The wall may have to be painted first with a suitable emulsion or decorator's colour to provide the right background. Alternatively, the wall can be covered with another material: lining paper or a similar paper available in a roll or large sheets; expanded polystyrene panels; hessian, burlap or an alternative fabric; flat or corrugated cardboard; pinboard or soft insulation board; hardboard (Masonite). A light wall covering such as paper, expanded polystyrene, thin fabric or cardboard, can be stuck to the wall with paste—a heavier one such as hessian, thick cardboard or board, with glue. Paste or glue the whole material or just enough of it to hold it in position. Some of the heavier boards may have to be fixed with wall plugs. Like the wall itself, these surfaces may need to be painted or textured first either before or after fixing them on the wall. Do whichever is more practicable.

Pieces for mounting direct onto a wall should stick easily and quickly: they are difficult to hold in place for long. Paste is fine for most materials, but some may need a gum or glue. Pieces that stand away from the wall must also take into account the lighting, which plays an important part in the final effect.

An alternative approach to wall design is to mount the pieces on a support flat on a table or floor and fix the support to the wall afterwards. The support should be made up to the largest size that is convenient to work on and fix up. For a paper support, paste roll-lengths or sheets together by their edges. When making a cardboard support, lay sheets edge to edge and glue strips of stout wrapping paper behind the meeting edges to join them. If pinboard, soft insulation board or hardboard are to be used, take the whole sheet or saw off as much as is required. If more than one sheet is to be used, lay them side by side for working on, and fix them to the wall one by one when the work is finished—unless it is possible to batten and manage them as one big piece from the start.

Work carried out in this way is often within easier reach and the pieces can be glued on at leisure, but it is not so easy to judge how the work as a whole is taking shape or how it will look in place, especially if this depends on lighting. The organizer has to decide which approach is more manageable.

b a model or construction
A group can also work together on a three-dimensional project, using any of the modelling and construction processes described in the book. A plan should be worked out first, in which it should be decided how the various parts are to be made and assembled. The plan can be followed closely or changes may be introduced as the work progresses. Alternatively, the work can grow spontaneously from the start as the contributions come together and develop an idea. Any structure needed for support should be prepared by as many as can conveniently help. The shape as a whole must be kept under review at every stage, and the latest shape borne in mind before any new piece is made up and added. Everyone should be able to share in finishing off the work.

Working independently

A group can make individual pieces for combining finally into a larger project. Each member of the group should know the overall intention behind the project and plan his work to fit into it. He should keep this in mind throughout, relating what he is doing to the work of others in the group, and putting his work with theirs from time to time to see that all is going well. There is more scope for personal ideas with this method, but always within the framework of the general aim: a single piece should not develop out of keeping with the rest. Any modifications needed should be made early on to avoid last-minute changes which could mean undoing earlier work. Points to watch out for to prevent this happening are the materials being used, the method of using them, and the relative sizes.

a   a wall design
As before, most of the flat and relief processes discussed earlier in the book can be used, though some, for example prints and made-up paper shapes, are more suitable than others. A theme or subject should be decided upon that will be suitable for the process chosen. The wall should then be prepared or the support made for mounting. Individuals make their own pieces as separate items, which are later assembled on the wall or support. This can be quite an exciting part of the project as the various pieces are tried out in different arrangements to fit together successfully. Themes such as 'Outer space', 'The insect world' or 'Happy crowd' would provide great scope.

b   a model or construction
Any of the modelling and construction processes may be used. The idea for a large-scale project should be discussed, and the particular process agreed on. Members of the group should work independently making their own contribution to it. As they will each be working alone, it is especially important that they keep an eye on what others are doing around them so that they conform to scale, colour and so on. Suitable themes include grouped figures, animals, objects, buildings, landscape features; sea, air and space subjects; incident or fantasy.

8 Suggested themes and topics

The following suggestions are offered merely as a guide to the kind of topics that might be developed from the different qualities and uses of paper. The only true guide, of course, is the individual's own response to the paper. The feelings and ideas arising from this are the real starting points, but it is sometimes helpful to have a few suggestions to open up the possibilities. The topics are listed under the various section headings.

Using paper flat

Torn and cut shapes
Movement or stillness of shapes
A crowd cheering
Flying
Invention for a cathedral
Northern Lights
Seaside houses
Cliff rescue
Procession to a shrine
Regions of the deep ocean
Invader of flowers
Crown of the emperors
Ghost ship

Collage
Movement and stillness of shapes
Feelings in a fairground
Surfaces to touch
East and West
Nearness of fire
Among ice and snow
Event in a city
Miracle worker
Wild creature
Inside a flower
Inside a jewel
Dream

Montage
Shapes in a new context
Bewildering moment
Mirage
In a cracked mirror
In the way of the wind
Earthquake
Unrecorded history
Sticking bills or posters
Beast to guard treasure

Creation of flowers
Object for speculation
Loss of memory

Counter-change
Reflecting shapes
Excited feeling
A sense of form
Light and shadow
Effects of a storm
Moonlit land
Decorating house fronts
Nearly twins
Penned livestock
Neighbours' flowers
Lightship
Impossible machinery

Silhouettes
A shape in contrast to its setting
Loneliness
Sense of menace
Behind bars
Sunshine and shadow
Skyline
Watching the fire
Leader
Night hunter
Desert cactus
Monument
Court of the chessmen

Mosaics
Design of fragments
Feeling gay
Sense of movement
A way through
Drifting snow

No coast for seamen
Excavating a lost city
Steeple-jack
Creature that travellers talk about
Corner of Eden
Ship of an invader
Seen under a microscope

See-through shapes
Design of dark and light shapes
Feeling at midnight
Behind the barricade
X-ray
Rain in the headlights
In a forest
Erecting a bridge
Miners at dawn
Caged animal
Wild plants against the sky
Satellite of the scientists
Magic lamp

Transparent shapes
Effects of transparency
Feeling cold
Afloat
Windows of the weatherman
Heatwave
Lake home
Descent of the astronauts
Diver
Bird at daybreak
Flower at twilight
The sultan's dome
Sea serpent

Projection slides
Design of transparent colours
Tranquility
A sense of space
Geometry of a star
Inside a rainbow
Primeval world
Firework
Dancer
Rare butterfly
Undiscovered flower
Strange toy
From an alien world

Prints with paper
Design of tones and colours
Running wild
Someone in the room
Coming into focus
Arctic twilight
Power station
Avalanche
Hooded ritual
Birds of prey
Plant without a name
Fossil
Mysterious cavern

Sandwich designs
Movement of line, tones and
    shapes
Carefree
Rhythm of a dance
Getting entangled
Tornado
Tunnels into the earth
Face to face encounter
Veiled figure
Creature yet to be born
Strange blooms
Discovered at the sea's edge
Goblin twins

Weaving
Design of tones and colours:
gay, restful, warm, cool,
contrasted, low-keyed, changing
in texture, ordered, free.

Stencils
Design of tones and colours
Frightened by shadows
Coming apart
Puzzle
Clouds and sunshine
Factory
Ploughing
Refugees
Creature of the wasteland
In the hothouse
Belfry
Ogre

Dip-dye designs
Design of tones and colours
Being in a crowd
Growing taller
Enclosed space
Misty morning
Mountains

Event for an insect
Queue
Wading birds
Forest
Map of an island
Mystic symbol

Using paper in relief

Crumpled
Design of varying relief areas
Calm and commotion
Surface inviting to touch
Trackless zones
Icy tundra
Houses in the old town
Rescue
Figure dressed for adventure
Armoured creature
Fungus family
Ancient stone circle
It came from outer space

Folded, rolled and curved
Design of relief shapes
Feelings in a strange place
On a journey
Entrances and exits
Change of weather
Home of the mathematician
Playing arcade machines
Inventor
Intruder at the hive
Unfolding blooms
Built for speed
No-one would believe it

Wave-formed
Design of undulating shapes
Exciting voyage
Moving freely
Turbulence
Incoming tide
Gentle land
Gale on wash day
Nun

Flying creature
Overgrown garden
Celebration flags
Temple of the Ocean God

Curled
Design of curled shapes
Unrest
Tensions
Echoes
Flames in the wind
Mill race
Collisions
Mermaid
Displaying bird
Climbing plant
Sea shell
Carnival fountains

Spiralled
Design of concave and convex
    forms
Design of raised spirals
Feelings in a fairground
Stairs to nowhere
Whirlwind
Rough sea
Spinning tops
Contortionist
Escaping creature
Seaweed
For scanning the skies
Arrivals on earth

Interlocked
Design of interlocked shapes
Design of woven shapes

Puzzled feeling
Sense of community
Idea for a game
Waterfall
Fly-over project
Friends
Beast of burden
Primeval forest
Maze
Temple of a lost faith

Ribboned
Design of ribboned shapes
Festive feeling
Rippling surface
Depths to explore
Blizzard
Entrance to a jungle
Trip down the rapids
Cavemen
Creature from the cold land
Mangrove swamp
Toy for the wind
The deluge

Landscaped
Design of landscaped forms
Everywhere to explore
Surface to shape shadows
Obstacles to development
Drifted dunes
Face of a future city
Playing a large instrument
Fighter
Monster
Petrified tree
Armoured vehicle
Machine for amusement

Pulped
Design of flat and relief surfaces
Unsettled feeling
The touch of contrasts
Plan for rehousing
Inferno
Unnavigable reaches
Felling a tree

Settler
Wild creature
Among plants
Excavating machine
Secret in the depths

Pasted in layers
Formed surface
Upheaval
Near to danger
Congestion
Meteorite
Strongroom
Flood
Weight-lifter
Creature of the rocks
Rare plant
In a museum
Coming of sleep

With metal foil
Design of metallic surfaces
Stillness
Pleasure of smooth planes
Patterns of a skater
Depths of space
Frozen north
In a submarine
Welder
Fish among currents
Rock plant
Treasure
Ghost galleon

With plaster
Irregular relief design
Feeling confused
Need for caution
Breaking up
Meteor storm
Landslide
Passage through the ice
Giant
Creature among corals
Old tree
Dug up from the past
The underworld

Using paper for modelling

Crumpled and tied
Contained or bound form
Under constraint
Sleep
Idea of the grotesque
A world in space
Boulder landscape
At the pantomime
Strange folk
Animal in action
Gourds
Cargo
Enchanted mushroom ring

Folded, rolled and curved
Plane form
Composed and still
Poised for action
Idea for a machine
Water over stone
Church
On the ski slopes
Organist
Ancient predator
Floor of the pinewood
Illuminated tower
Home of the wizard

Curled and spiralled
Rhythmic form
Feeling giddy
In motion
Tensions
Breaking waves
Floor of an ocean
Working a lathe
Snake charmer
Shell-fish
Twining plant
Spiral stairway
New game

Interlocked
Keyed form
Getting involved
Trapped
Without an end

Air turbulence
Tower for viewing
Mechanical earth mover at work
Embrace
Heraldic beast
Tangled growth
Labyrinth
Game

Ribboned
Form from strands
High spirits
Sense of freedom
Disorder
Heavy rain
Waterfall
Explosion
Hermit
Creature from the cold land
Trailing plant
Gay tents
Maypole mix-up

Landscaped
Plane form
Instinct to dominate
Stability
Stock-piling
Stalagmite
Volcanic island
Vintage car race
Crusader
Protected animal
Fallen tree
Rock crystal
Guardian angel

See-through forms
Form with openings
Feeling vulnerable
Inviting exploration
Fragility
Frost
Crane over building site
Night work in office
  block
Bride

Nesting bird
Thicket
Memorial
Device to trap shadows

Transparent forms
Form of transparent colours
Gaiety
Spell-bound
Idea for a gem
Path through a rainbow
Place to dream in
Inside a sunset
Teller of fortunes
Life in the deep
Miracle of a flower
Throne
Hallowe'en

Pulped
Modelled or supported form
All alone
Poised
Taking a load
Melting in fire
Primitive home
Obstacle race
Prospectors
Creature in a cave
Vegetable plot
Cromlech
Death in the desert

Pasted in layers
Modelled or constructed form
In love
Off-balance

For transmitting signals
Planet passing near
Quarry
Rocket launch
Stunt flier
Trapped animal
Growing by a stream
Found in the attic
Devil scarer

Metal foil forms
Metallic form
Moving smoothly
In a crush
Deceptive weight
Passing spheres
Among ice-floes
In the operating theatre
Astronomer
Battle of the big fish
Plant and insect
Sealed in an Egyptian tomb
Belonging to the Small Folk

Paper and foil casts
Irregular form
Sense of the uncreated
Inviting touch
Effects of time
Eruption
Among the tors
Demolishing a building
Wild figure
Dinosaur
Decay in the woods
From under the sea
Mysterious growth

Working in a group

Working together

a
Design of colour and texture
   surfaces
Mixed feelings

Being in space
Wall of mystic symbols
Weather forecast

Land for adventure
Creation
Return of a hero
Wild sanctuary
Forgotten garden
Transport museum
Dreams of many sleepers
b
Assembled form
Congestion

Growing bigger
Look-outs everywhere
Catching fire
Refinery
Japanese wrestling match
One-man band
Procession elephant
Homes in the old tree
Old steam roller
In the cave of vampires

Working independently

a
Design of colour and relief
  surfaces
Surprise
Falling
Hunger
Treasury of the rocks
Passages
The uprising
Survivors
Animals marooned in floods
Botanists' paradise
In the antique market
Meeting of magicians

b
Assembled forms
Transfixed with fear
Feeling one's way around
Emerging
Whirled in the storm
Settlement
Race for life
Resting in the heat
The herd
Multiplying underground
At an auction
The next world

Further reading

d'Arbeloff, N. and Yates, J. *Creating in Collage* Studio Vista, London 1967; Watson–Guptill, New York

British Paper and Board Makers' Association *Paper making. A general account of its history, processes and applications* 1949

Grater, M. *Make it in Paper* Mills and Boon, London, 6th imp 1969; Taplinger Publishing Co., Inc., New York, 1962

Grater, M. *Paper People* Mills and Boon, London, 1969

Harbin, Robert *Teach yourself Origami, the art of paper folding* English Universities Press, London, 1968

Hartung, R. *Creative Corrugated Paper Craft* Batsford, London, 1966; Van Nostrand Reinhold, New York, 1966

Hawkesworth, E. *The Art of Paper Tearing* Faber and Faber, London, 1970

Hickman, Peggy *Silhouettes* Cassell, London, 1968

Honeywood, Mary *Making Pictures in Paper and Fabric* Batsford, London, 1968; Watson–Guptill, New York, 1969

Kuo, N. *Chinese Paper Cut Pictures* Tiranti, London, 1964

Lipski, Tadeusz *Paper Sculpture* Studio, London and New York, 1947

Lorrimer, Betty *Creative Papier Mâché* Studio Vista, London, 1971; Watson–Guptill, 1972

Norris, F. *Paper and Paper Making* Oxford University Press, London, 1952

Portchmouth, John *Creative Crafts for Today* Studio Vista, London, 1969; Viking Press, New York, 1969

Randlett, S. *The Art of Origami* Faber and Faber, London, 1963

Röttger, E. *Creative Paper Craft* (U.S. *Creative Paper Design*) Batsford, London, 1961; Van Nostrand Reinhold, New York

Sadler, A. *Paper Sculpture* Blandford, London, 1964

Index